Look Up Mississippi

My Backyard Garden

Photo Memoir and “Way In The Middle of the Air” Poem

Debra Hester

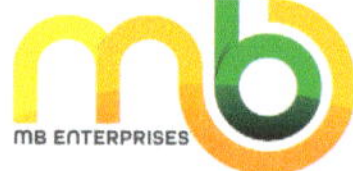

My Backyard Garden - Look Up Mississippi.

The opinions expressed in this manuscript are solely the opinions of the author. The author has represented and warranted ownership and legal right to her personal photos included. Public domain photos included in artwork show reference to original source. Any references, suggestions, recommendati ons or experiences implied or stated are based on the author's perspective and not intended as a factual reference but as a reflective, editorial experience.

MB Enterprises - www.mothersbackyard.com (Mother's Backyard Enterprises)

Library of Congress Control Number: 2020924419

Paperback ISBN: 978-1-7361463-0-9.

Printed in the United States of America

Table of Contents

Dedication

My Backyard Garden, Look Up Mississippi is dedicated to the memory of two extraordinary scholars. Their names are Yvette Danley and Robert Kinchen. We all went to Central High School in Helena-West Helena, Arkansas during forced integration in the mid-nineteen seventies.

Yvette and Rob were the first African Americans that I knew personally who came from my small home town along the Arkansas side of the Mississippi River and went to an Ivy League university. They both attended Harvard University in the mid 70's. As their underclassperson in high school, I was amazed by their kind, humble and fun demeanor; yet powerful academic performance.

While they moved to other parts of the U.S.A., they never forgot where they came from. They were not proud, boastful or rude. From my account they were also very courageous to venture so far, so fast, so young and hit their target like an eagle. Yes, they both graduated from Harvard University. Yvette with an Engineering Degree and Rob with a Law Degree in 1978. They both passed on in 2020.

I do believe they did "look up."

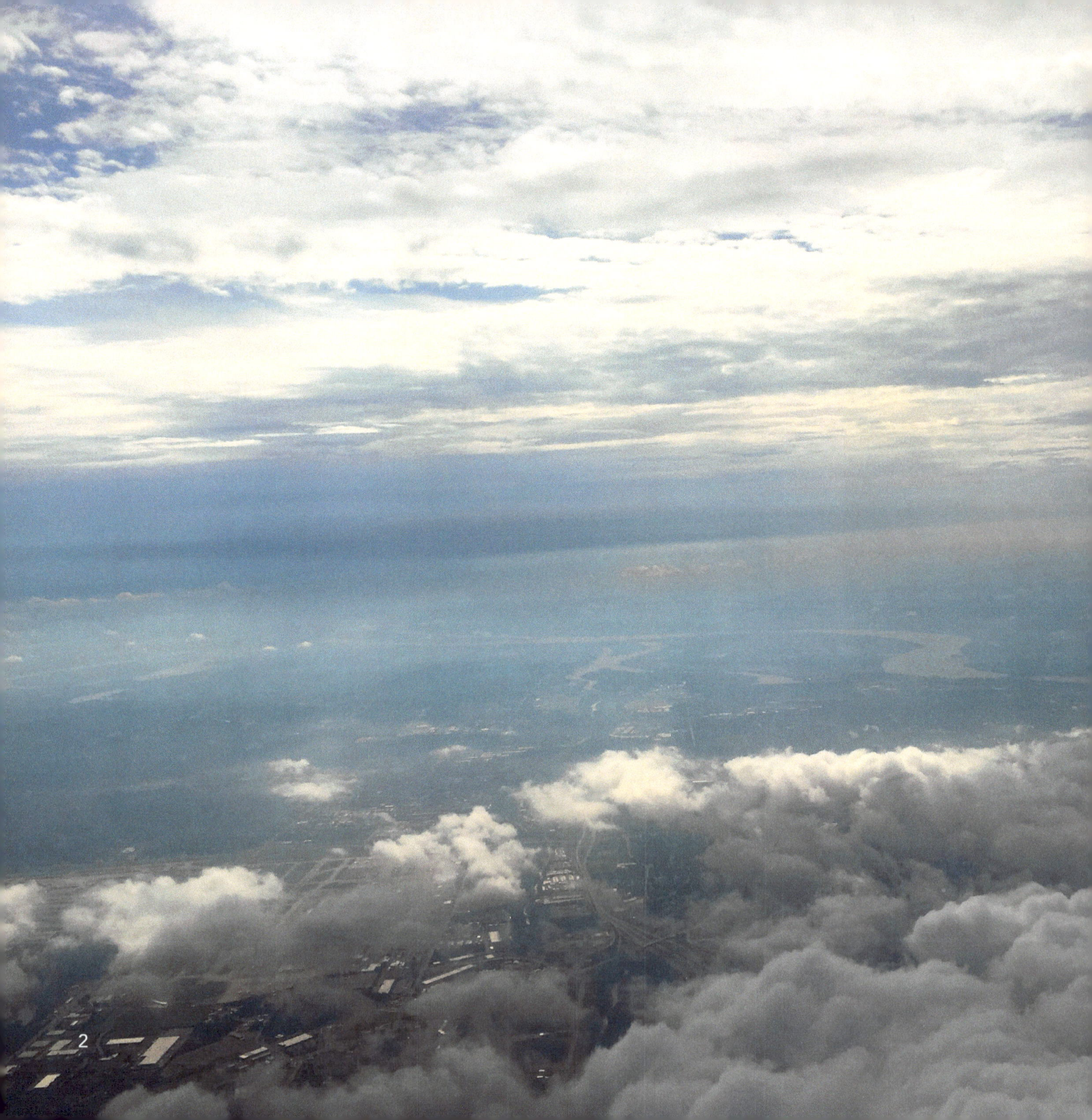

Reflective Meditation

"Whenever the living beings moved, the wheels moved with them. And whenever the living beings rose from the earth, the wheels rose also. Wherever the spirit was about to go, they would go in that direction. And the wheels rose close beside them; for the spirit of the living beings was in the wheels."

The Book of Ezekiel 1:19-20

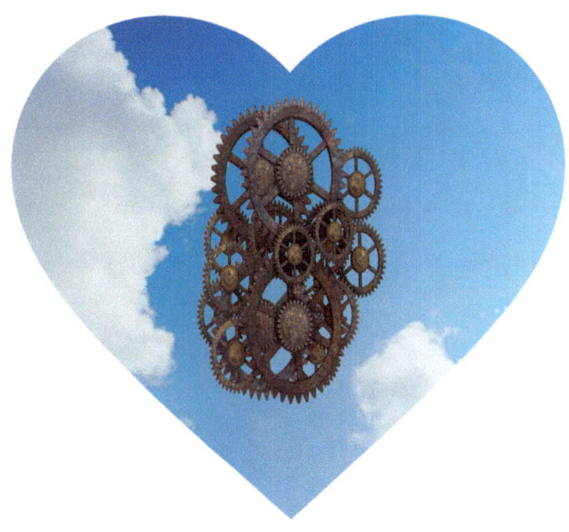

Wheel Photo: Image by Susann Mielke from Pixabay with MB Design

Introduction

Welcome to *My Backyard Garden, Look Up Mississippi,* a landscape memoir.

I am grateful for the timing of this collection. It commemorates the changing of the Mississippi State flag that is named the "In God We Trust" flag and the "Magnolia Flag."

I consider ***MBG*** - ***Look Up Mississippi*** an inspirational picture book that captures some of Mississippi's natural beauty. I have often found condolences in the clouds, skies, rivers and streams regardless of what might be happening in the world. I randomly captured these photos over the past five years. These photos helped me remember to be grateful for what does exist versus dwelling on what does not exist. The Universe presented the perfect time to share them with you.

I'm not a native of Mississippi. However, my grandmother and great-grandmother came from this eastern side of the Mississippi River into Arkansas, where I was born. Relatives from Mississippi include the Wynn and Kilgore families.

During my childhood and as a young adult, Mississippi had a terrible reputation for how it treated African Americans, along with other minority groups. So, I wasn't surprised when, after forty years away from the South, everyone, regardless of color or age, was surprised when I said I was moving back to the South and to Mississippi.

Some of my family was part of the Great Northern Migration in the early 20th century. Historians report that the Great Migration saw over 6 million African Americans move from the South to the North, Midwest, and West between 1910 and 1970. However, some stayed, others tried the North and then returned to the South. My generation headed West. My sites were on moving west to California. As a young woman, I did move West with a stop in Oklahoma and Arizona.

Some of us came back to the South. Our coming back did not make the news like Deion Sanders' acceptance as head coach for Jackson State University located in the capital of Mississippi. However, his move and our move confirmed my hope and vision for a better and different state. Maybe we saw "the wheels."

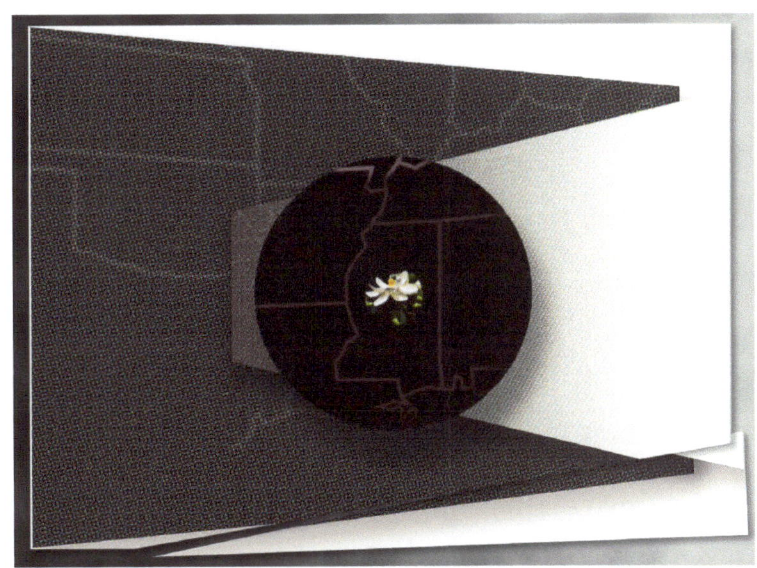

Southern Magnolia Pixabay photo by Jalynn Mississippi, U.S.A. - The Magnolia State, an MBE Design

Why I Created this Book

Mississippi received a reputation that many states should have received. Technology has revealed the deep-seated racism that exists in every region of our country and the world. We didn't see that such hatred still existed until recently, but I believe this is a period of uncovering many unknowns.

So if you have never ventured to set foot in Mississippi, here are some views of mostly the skies. If skies are not your thing, there is excellent fishing, eating, music and history here too. After living on both the East and West Coast, the Mississippi Coast was like a fresh breath of unpolluted air. From Gospel to Country, to Rhythm and Blues to Zydeco, I'll bet one of the state's original music forms will make you dance, laugh or cry.

It's inspirational to me, and I hope to you and this state's future as we remove in 2020 the confederate symbol that has been on the state's flag since 1861. As we officially raise the new flag in 2021, I'm sure "Ezekiel saw the wheels, way up in the middle of the air" will continue to drift through my mind. So, as I share these images, don't be surprised if the spiritual song surfaces in your mind, too, as you peruse the content.

Having the chance to publish this photographic memoir brings me so much joy and satifaction that our world is growing in empathy, compassion, love and respect.

As a child, I spent countless days looking at these skies. What as a child brought me anxiety, as Mother, Aunt M and Aunt L rushed to drive home from Memphis, Tennessee to Helena, Arkansas through Mississippi before dark, I might add, now brings me peace. Now, these skies bring not only peace but expectation every day. See how things can change for the better if we just continue to move forward and look up.

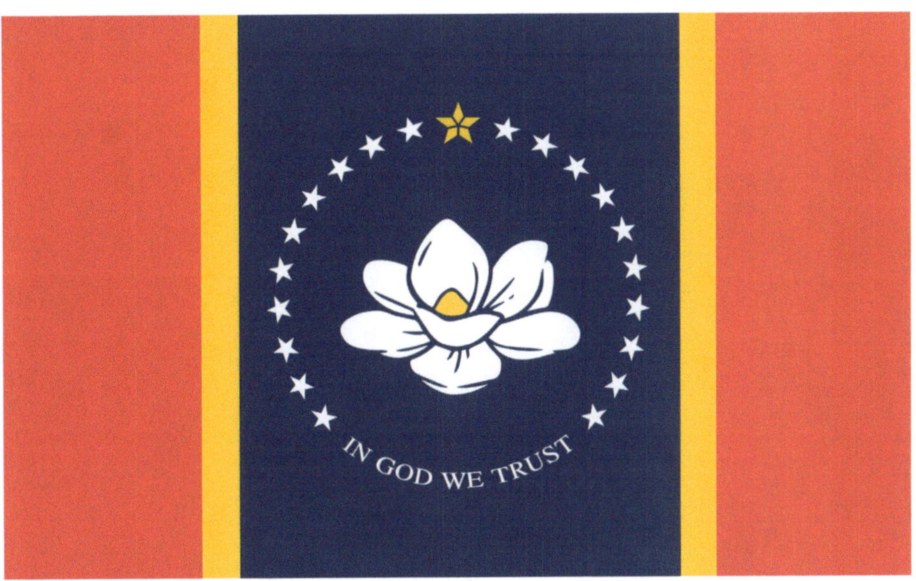

The flag of Mississippi features a white magnolia blossom and the words "In God We Trust" on a red field with a gold-bordered blue pale. This flag was chosen by the Commission to Redesign the Mississippi State Flag and was approved by state referendum on November 3, 2020. Afterward, it was passed by the state legislature on January 6, 2021, and it became the official state flag of the U.S. state of Mississippi on January 11, 2021.[2][3][4] Govenor of Mississippi, Tate Reeves. The flag was designed by Rocky Vaughan, Sue Anna Joe, Kara Giles, Dominique Pugh, and Micah Whitson. Information obtained at: https://en.wikipedia.org/wiki/Flag_of_Mississippi

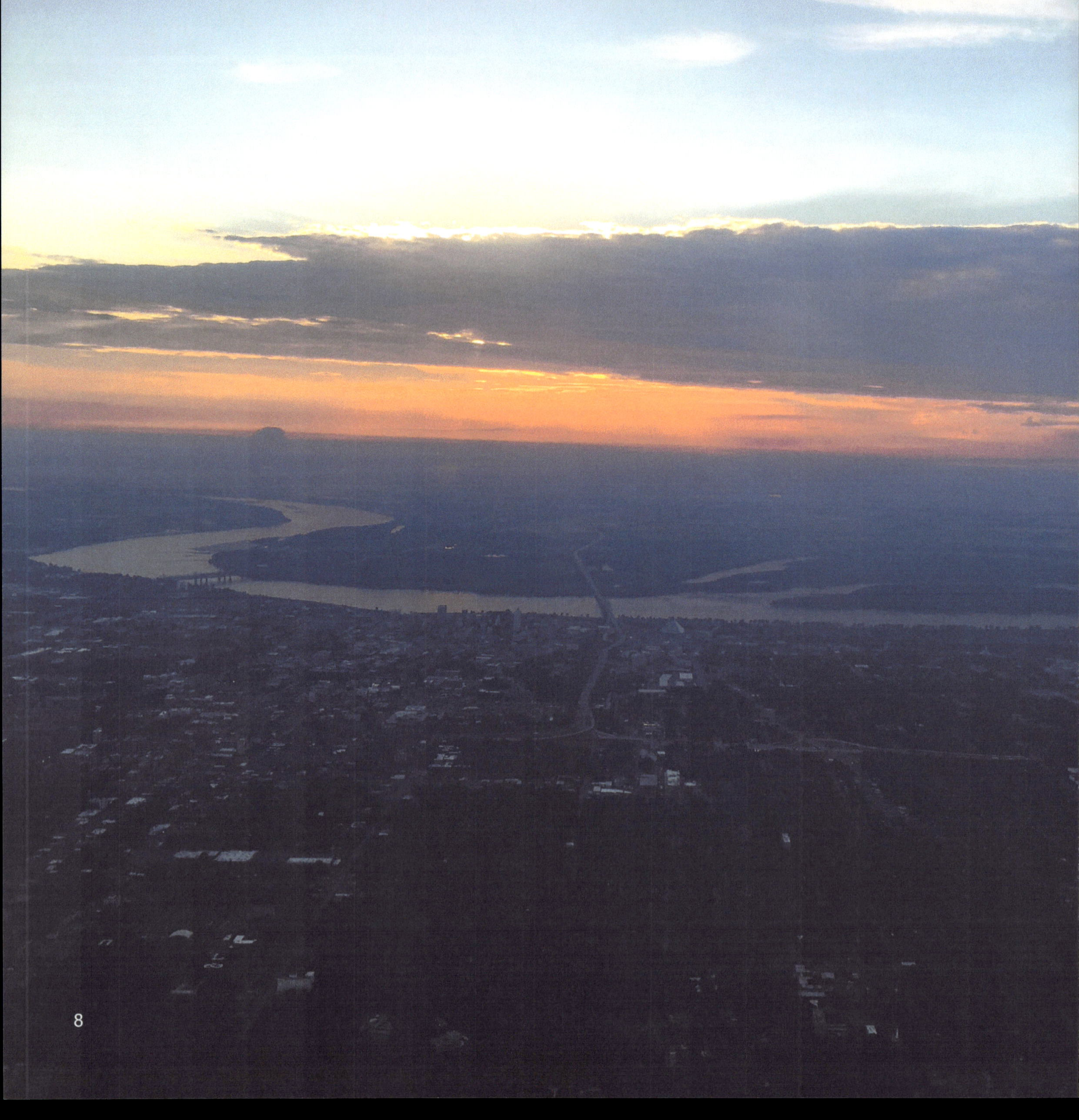

1

MISSISSIPPI WATERWAYS

Returning to the Delta as an adult helped me remember why I sat and starred at the skies so much as a child. They're captivatingly beautiful in this part of the country.

Maybe it's due to its proximity to the mighty Mississippi River that barrels through this fertile land. My photos only have titles. I'll leave the rest to your imagination and reflection.

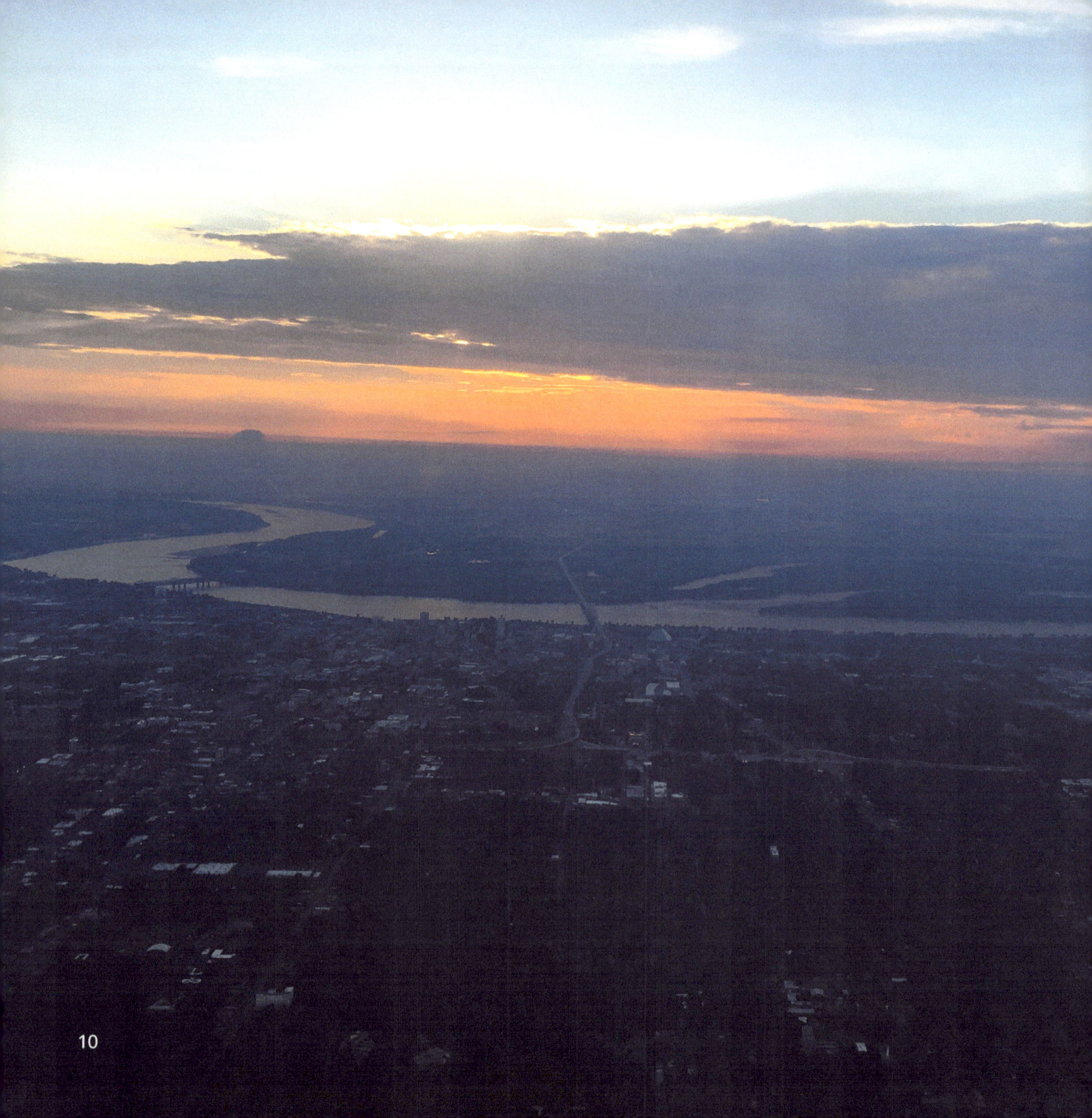

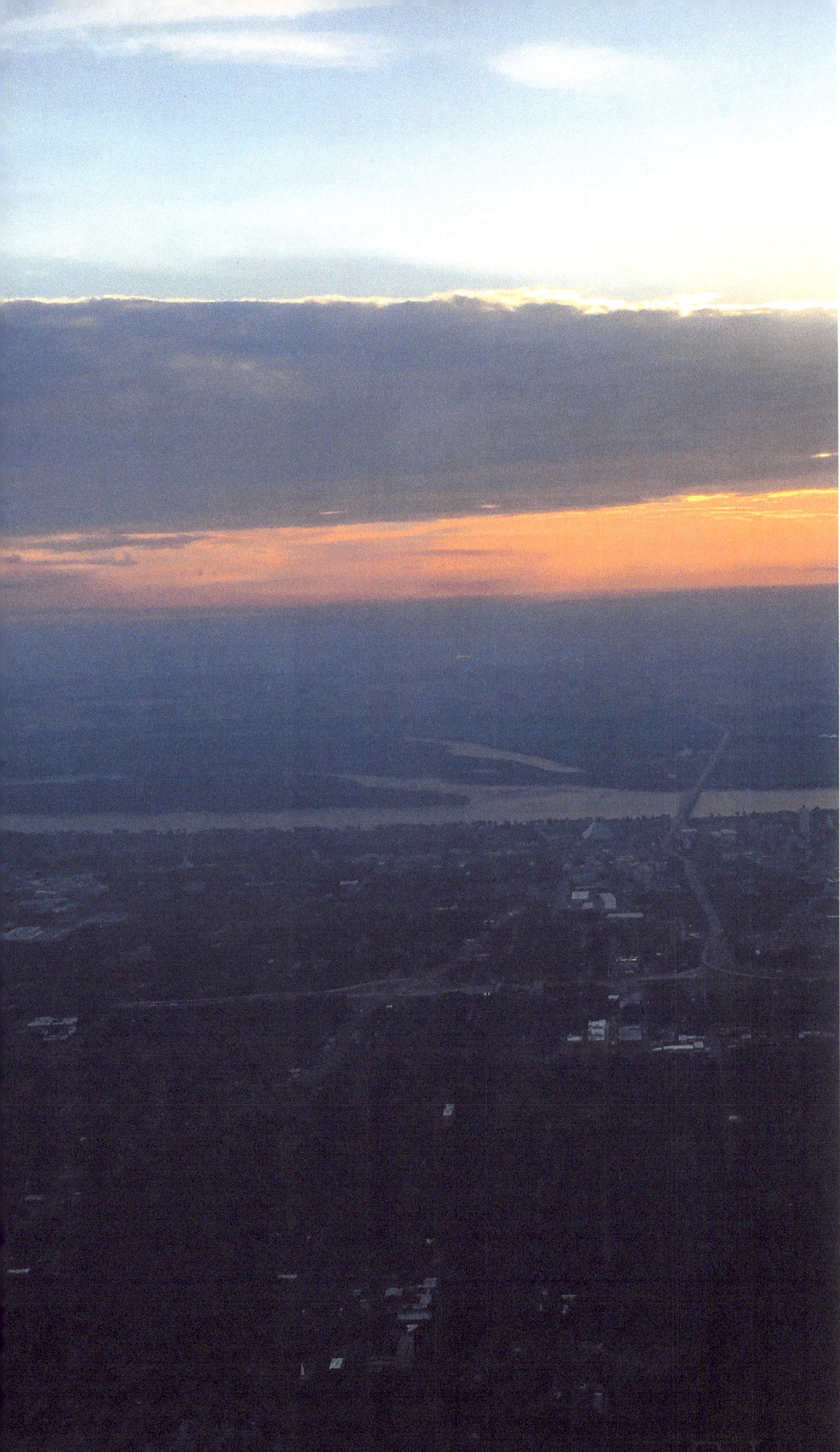

Father of Waters

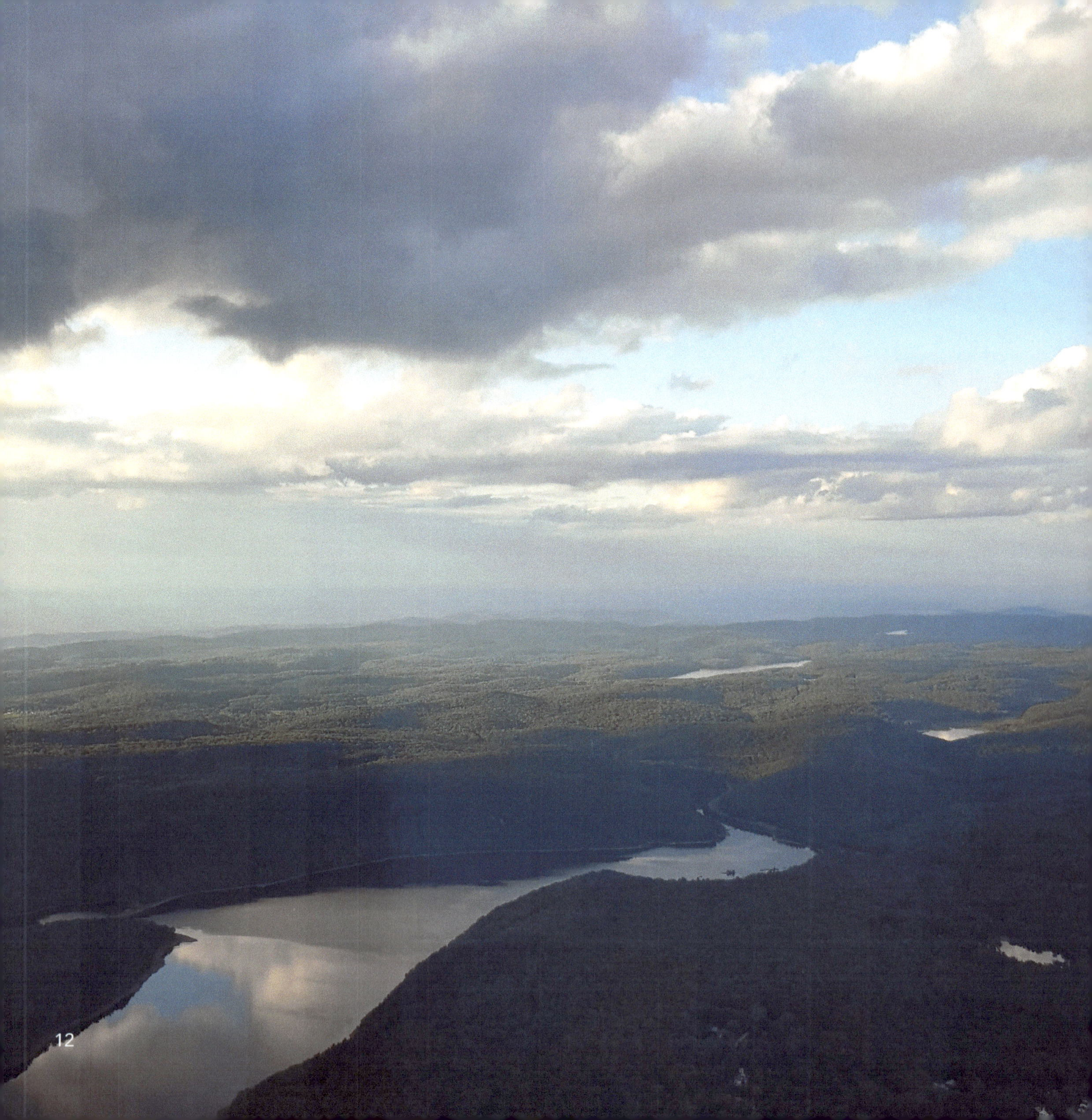

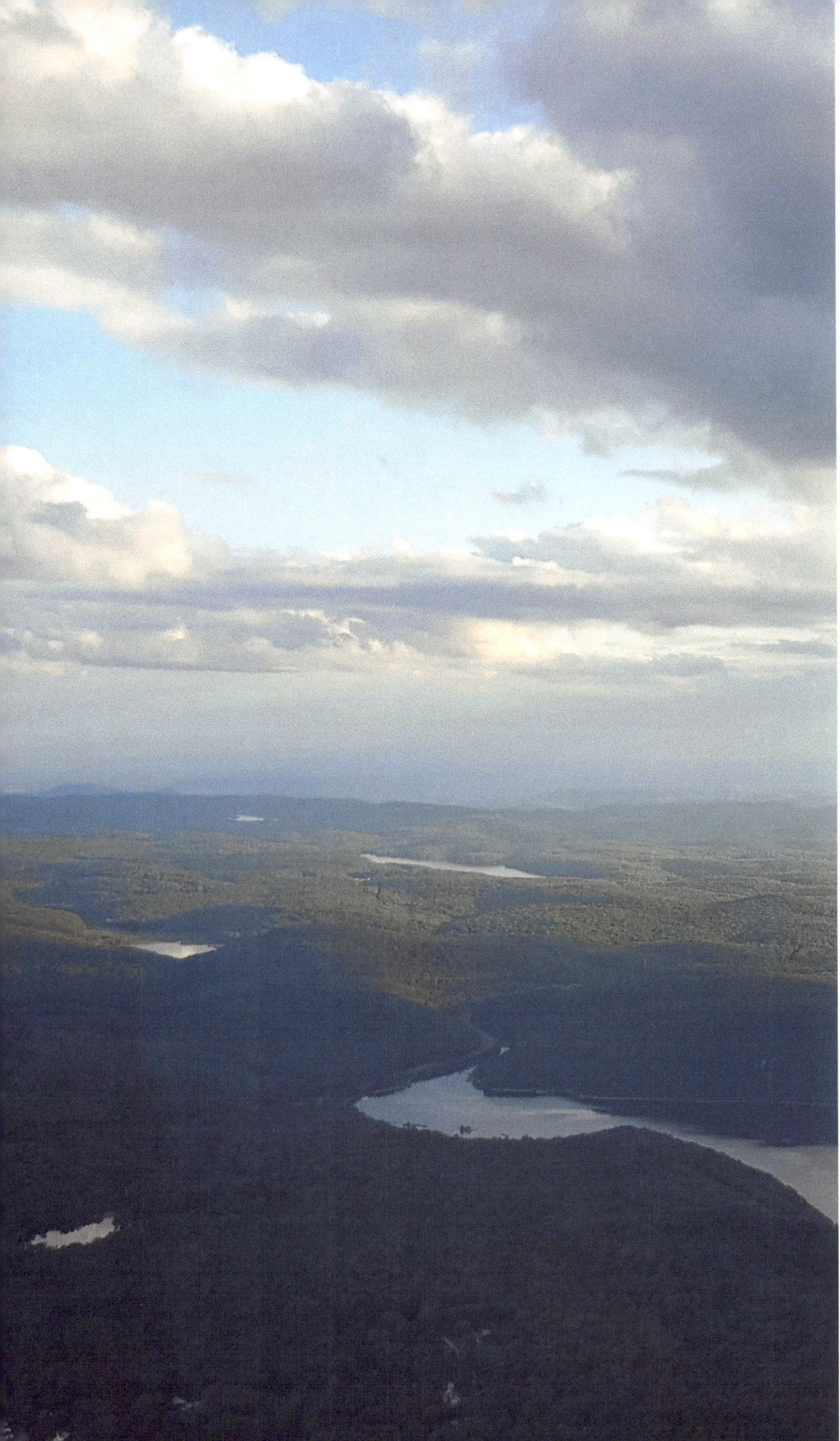

River Reflections

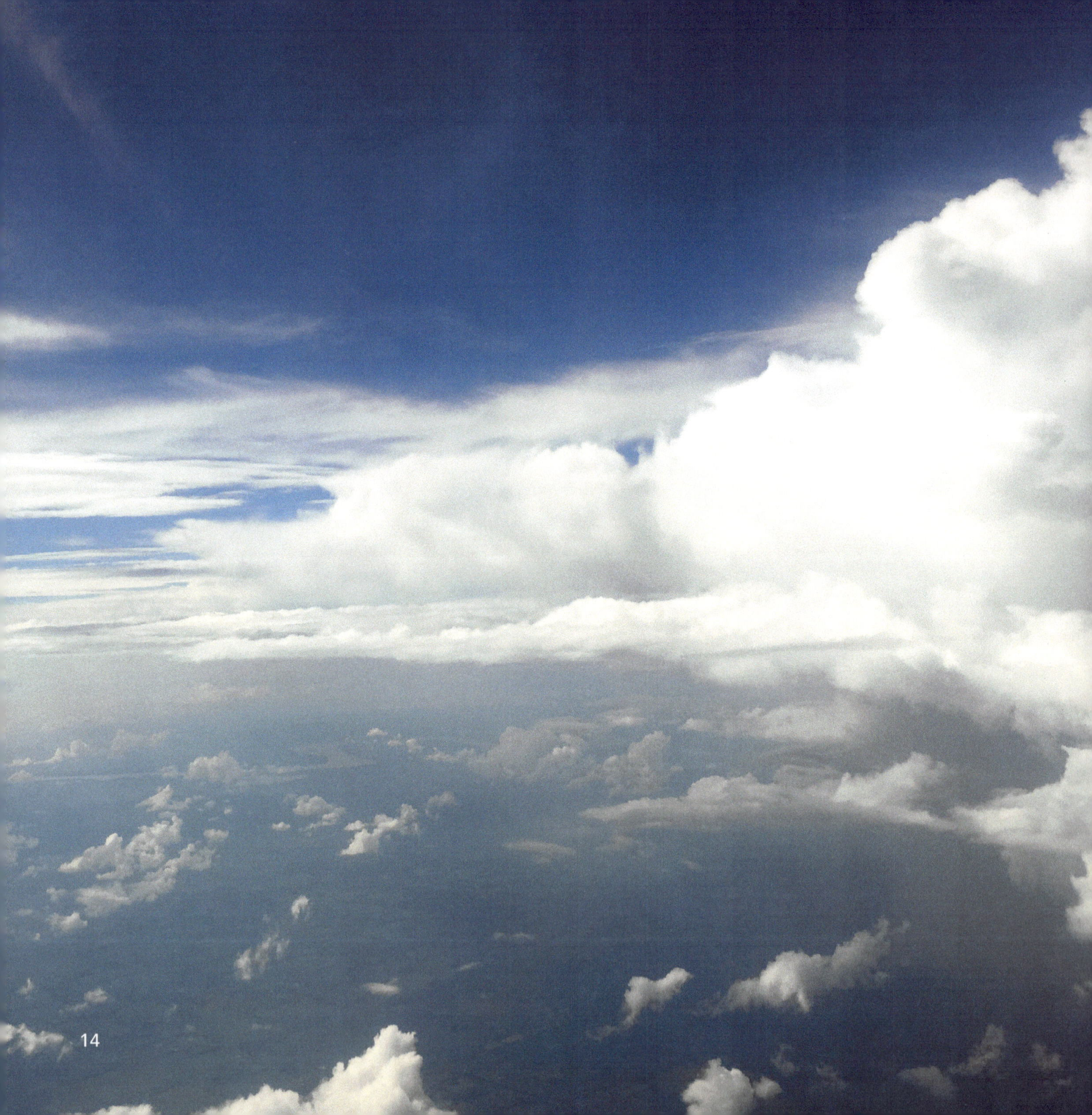

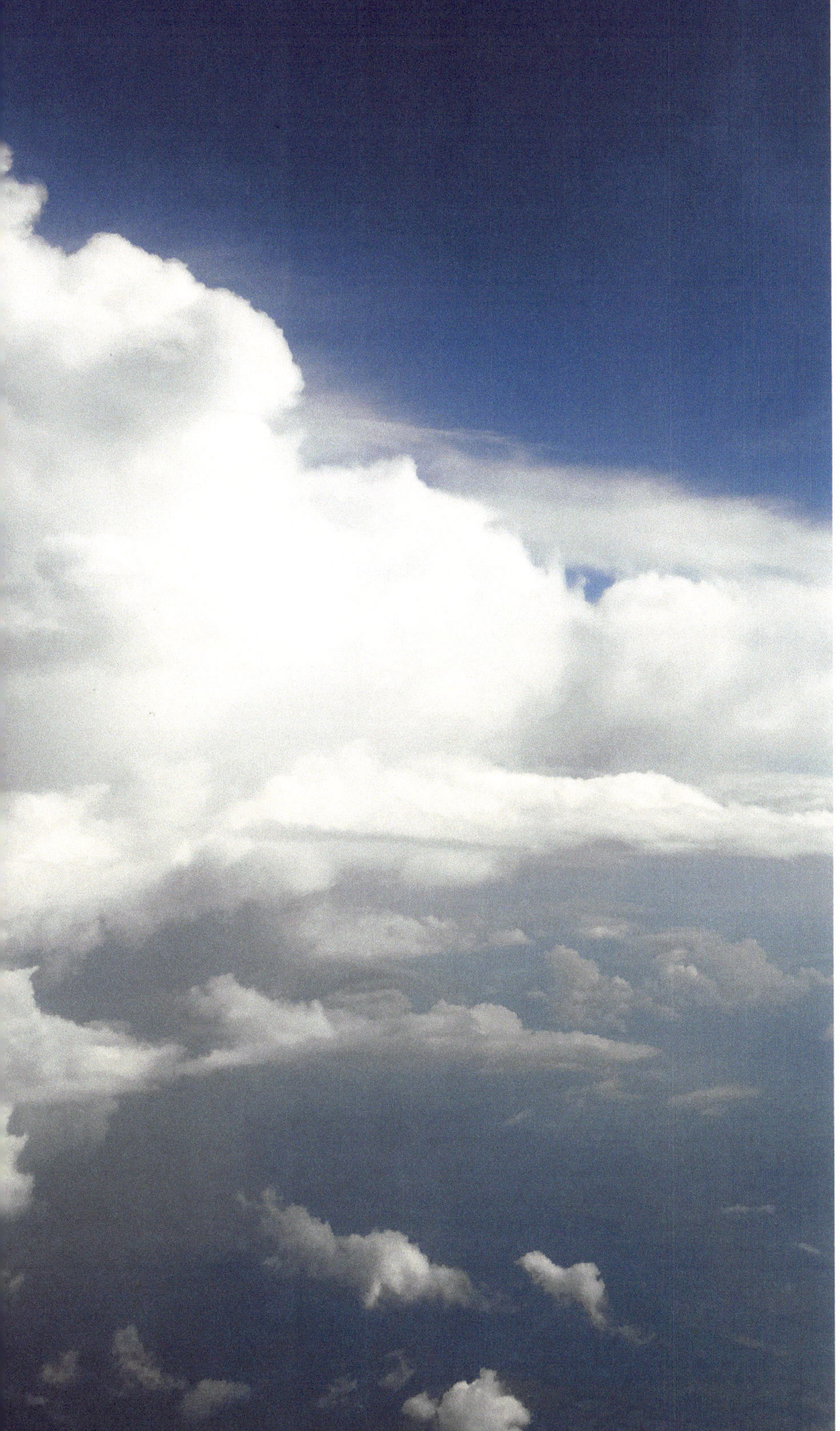

Uplifting

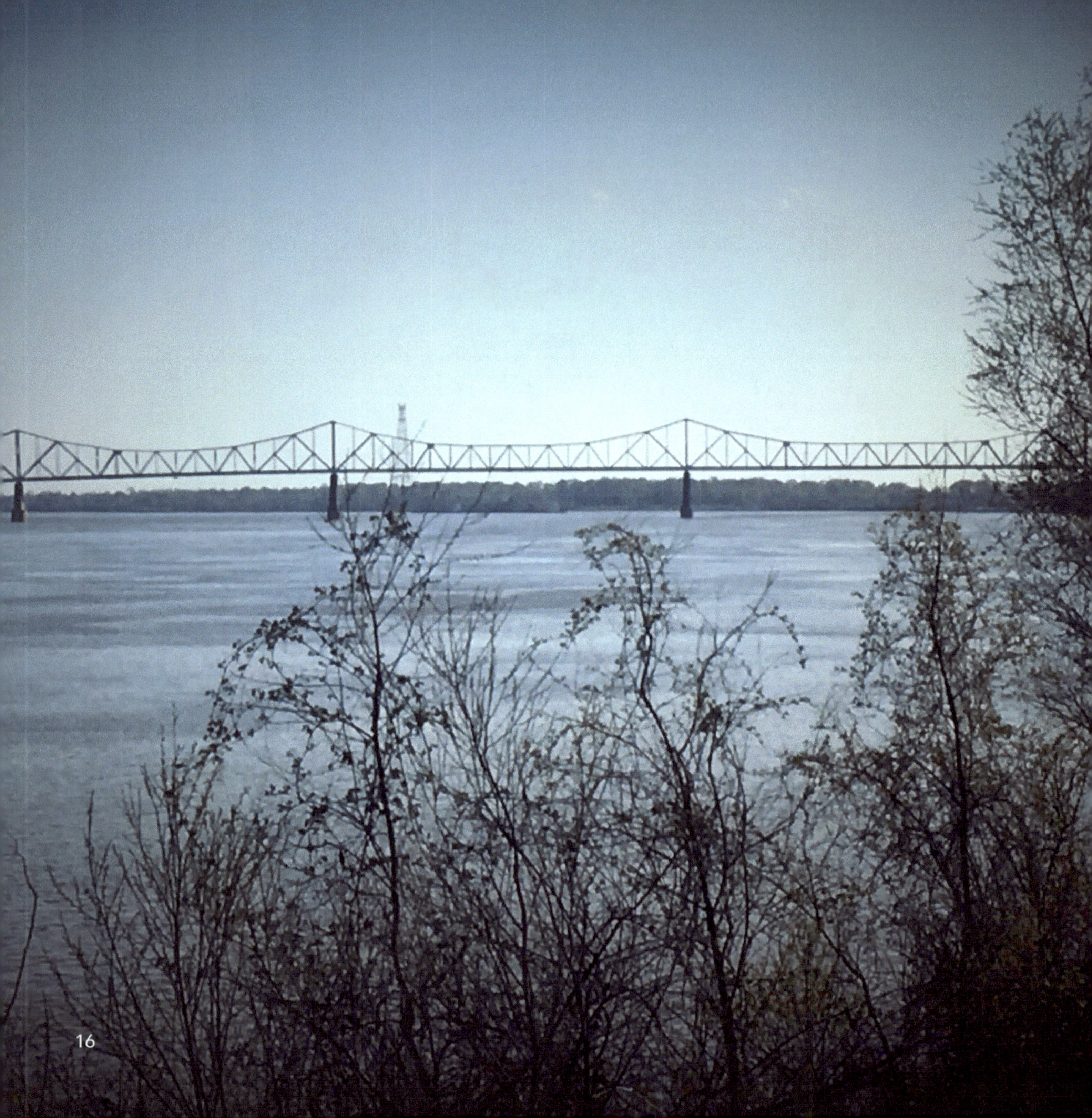

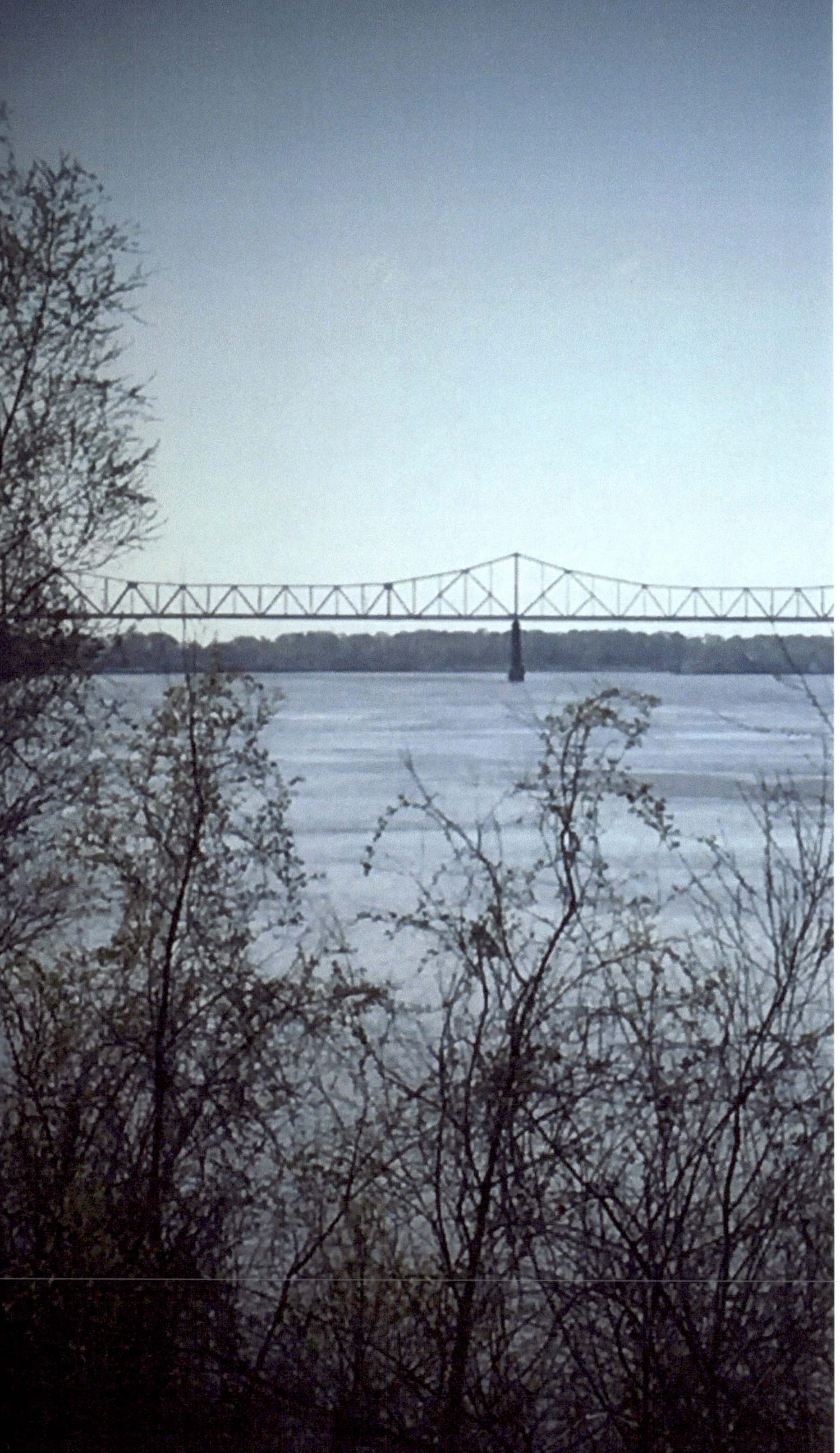

The Bridge Home

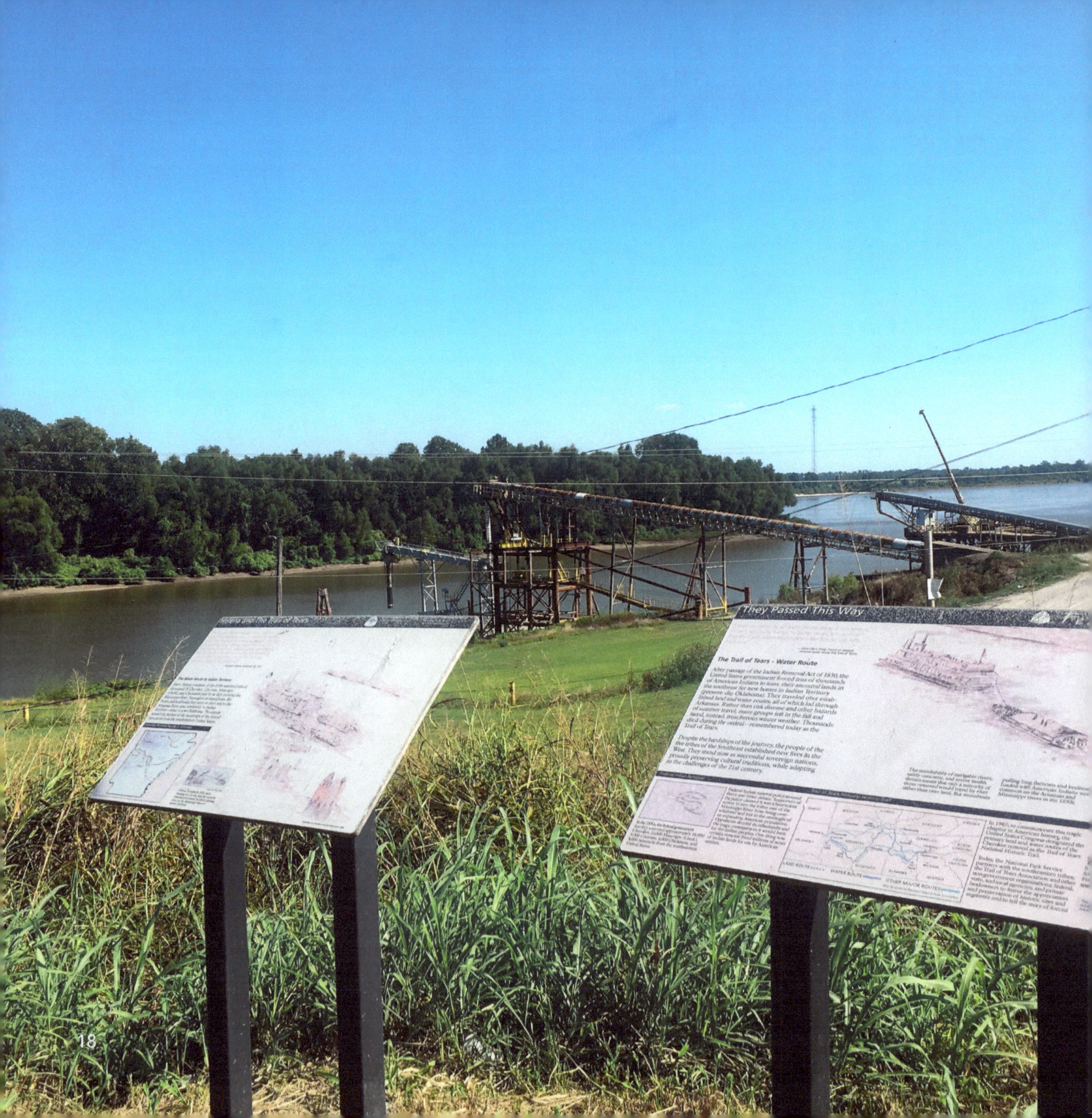
They Passed This Way
The Trail of Tears - Water Route
After passage of the Indian Removal Act of 1830, the United States government forced tens of thousands of American Indians to leave their ancestral lands in the southeast for new homes in Indian Territory (present-day Oklahoma). They traveled over established land and water routes, all of which led through Arkansas. Rather than risk disease and other hazards of summer travel, many groups left in the fall and faced, instead, treacherous winter weather. Thousands died during the ordeal—remembered today as the Trail of Tears.
Despite the hardships of the journey, the people of the five tribes of the Southeast established new lives in the West. They stand now as successful sovereign nations, proudly preserving cultural traditions, while adapting to the challenges of the 21st century.

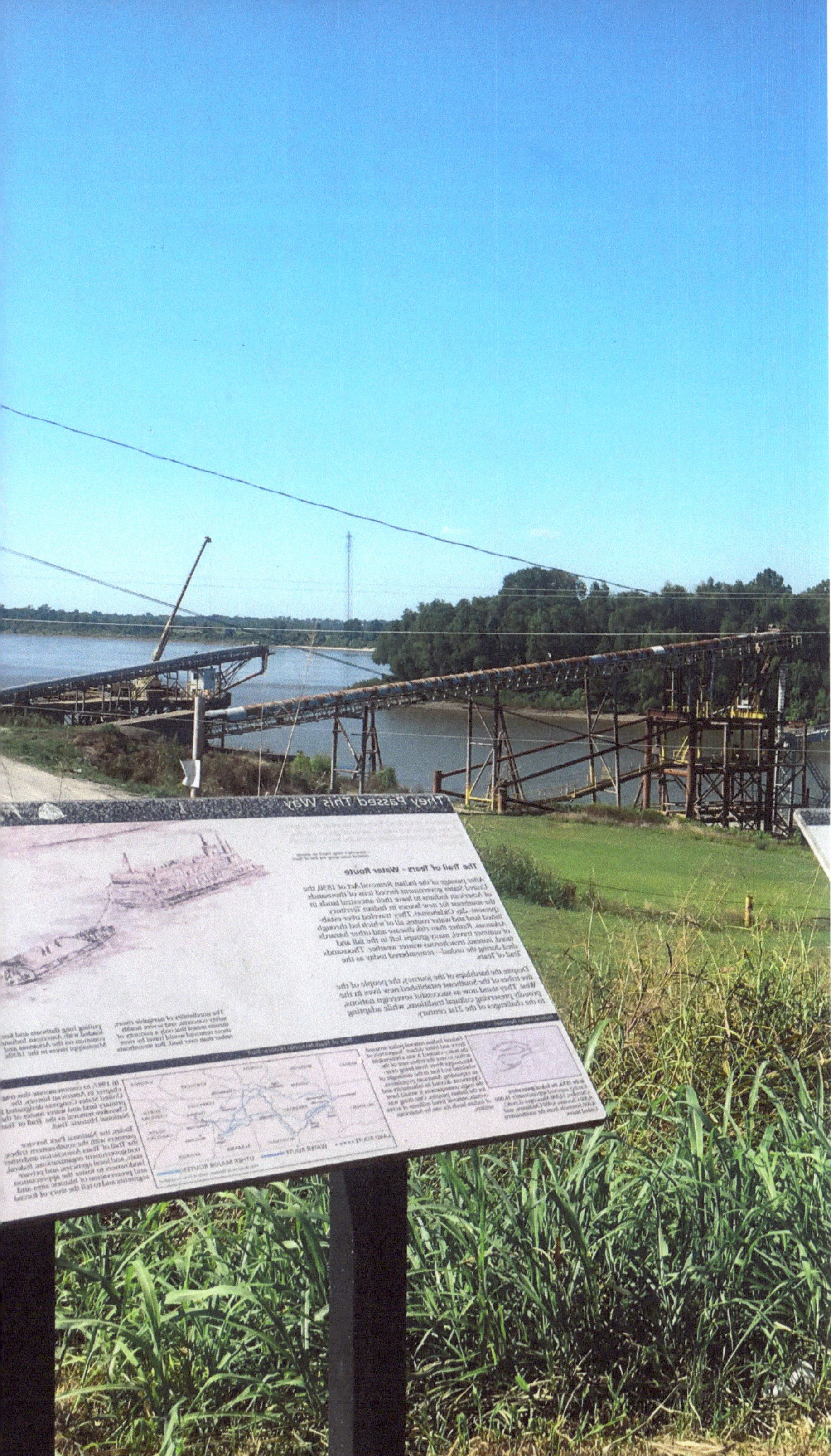

River Work

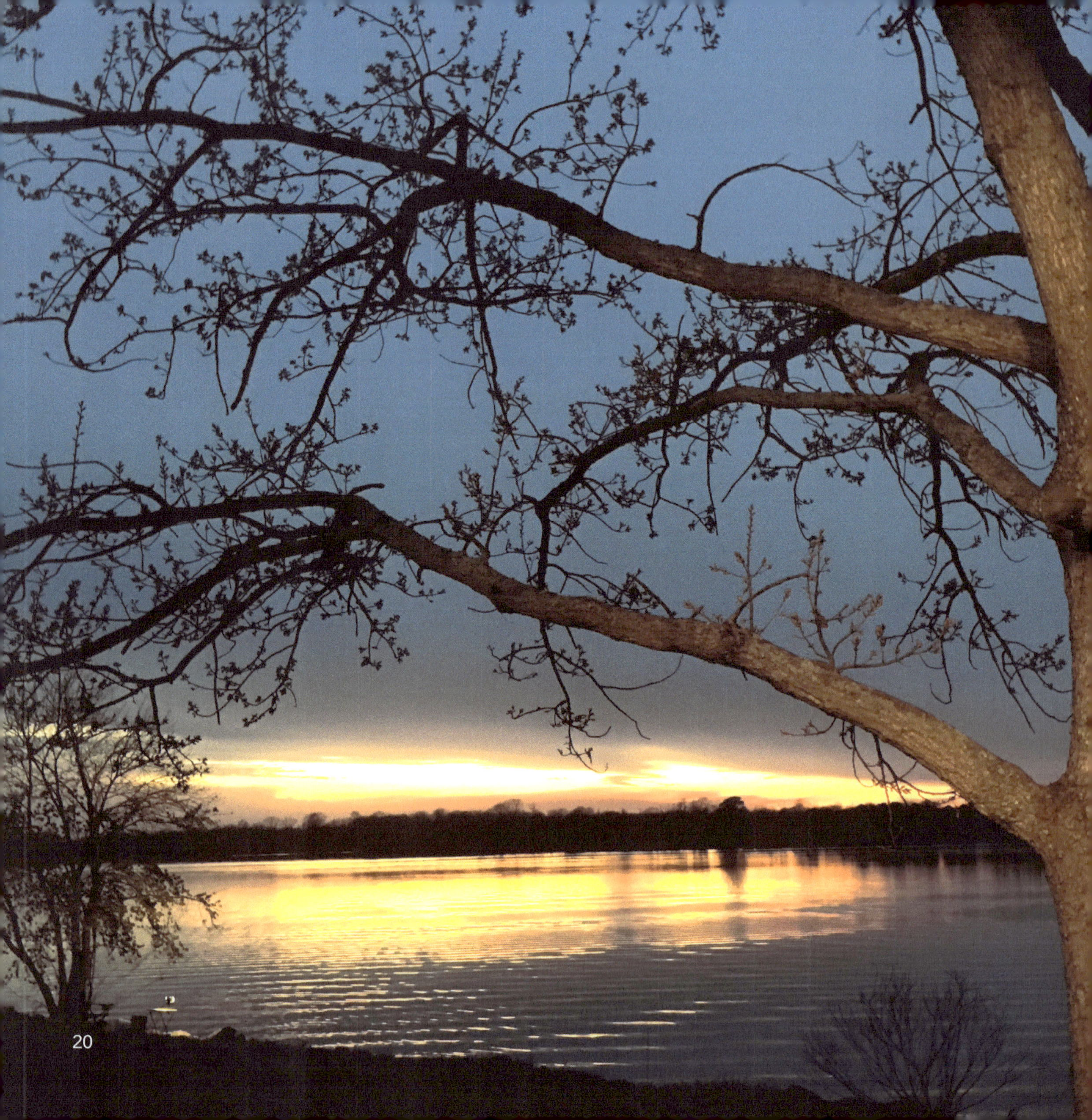

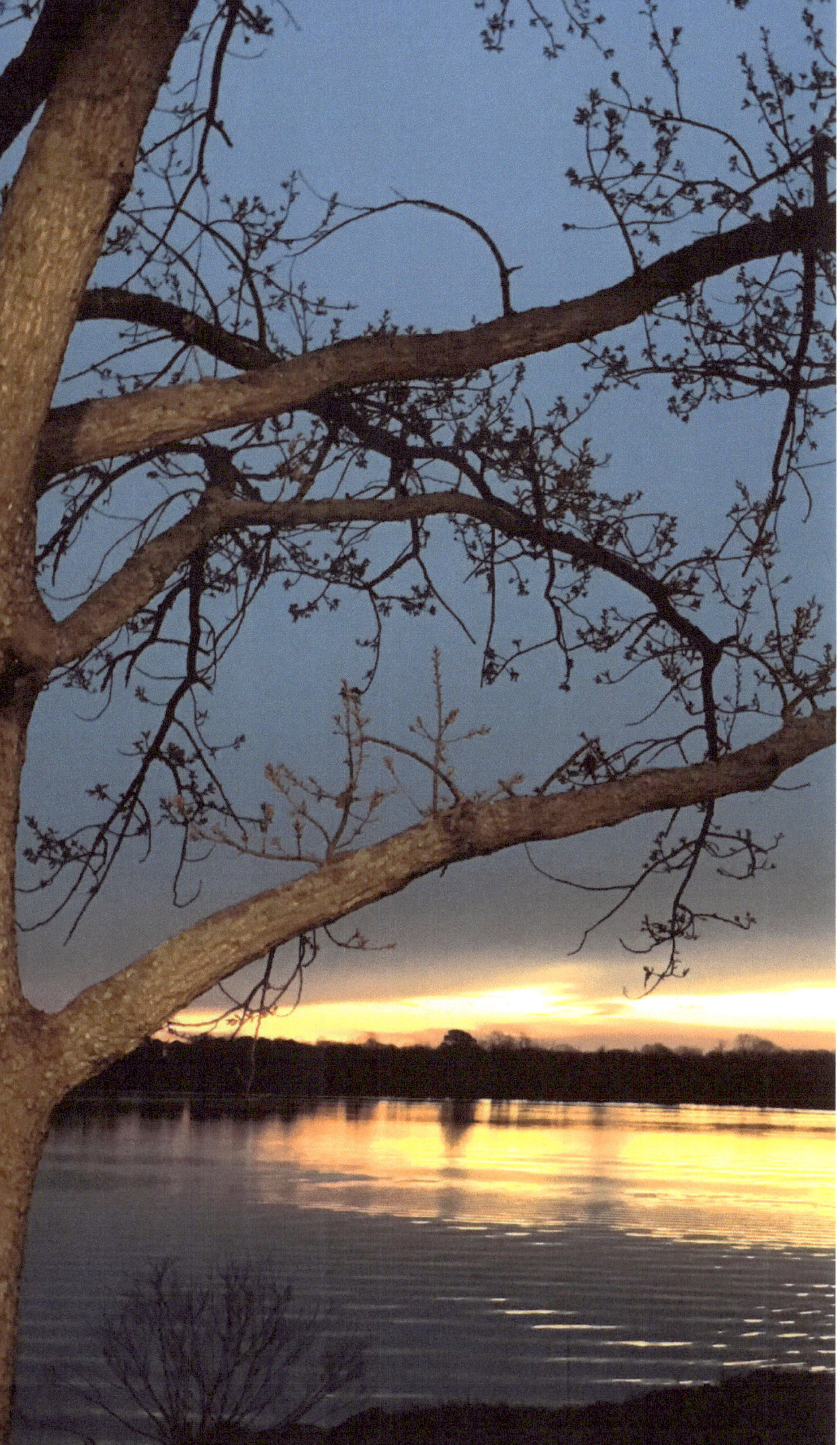

Lavender Ripples

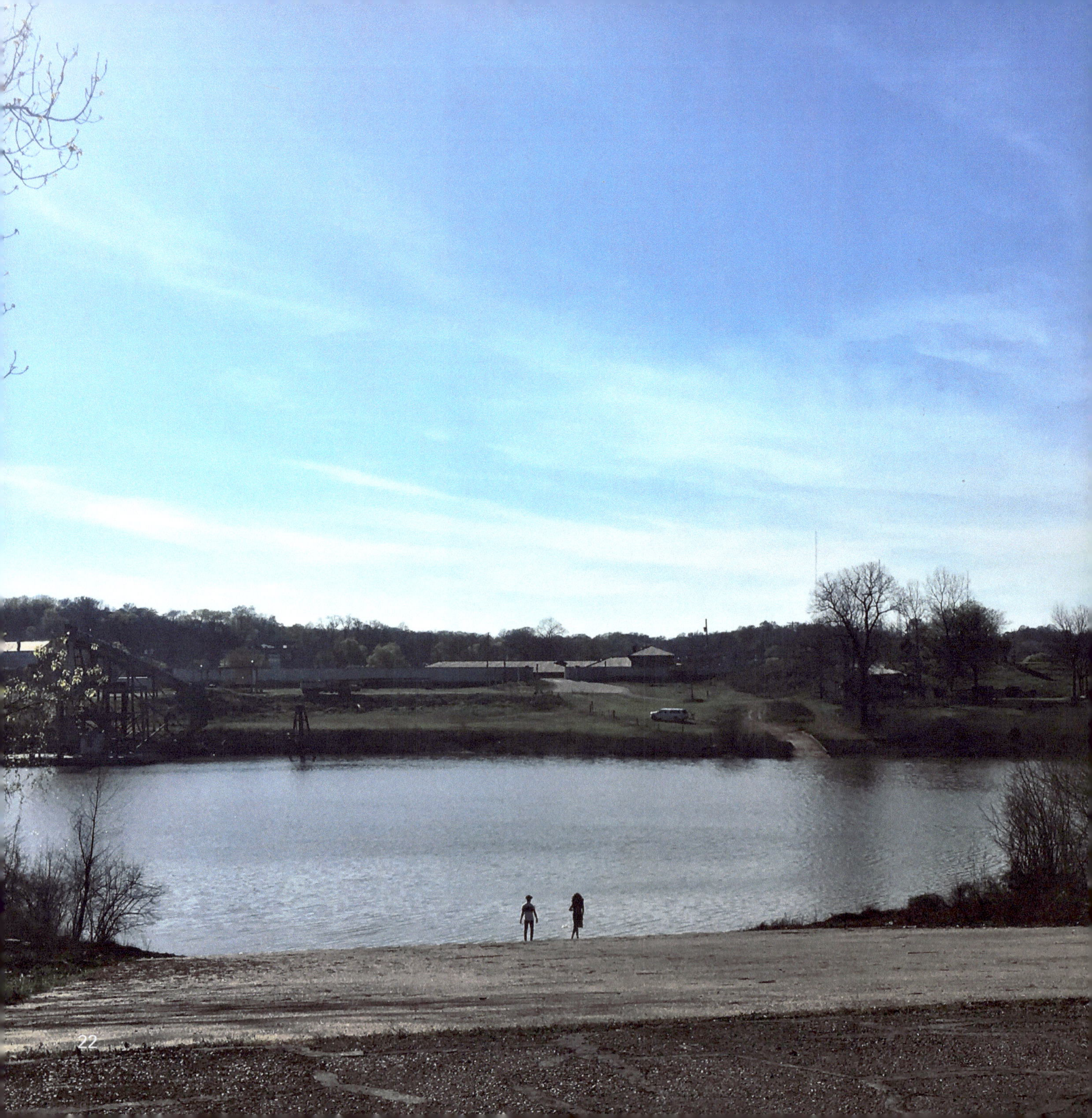

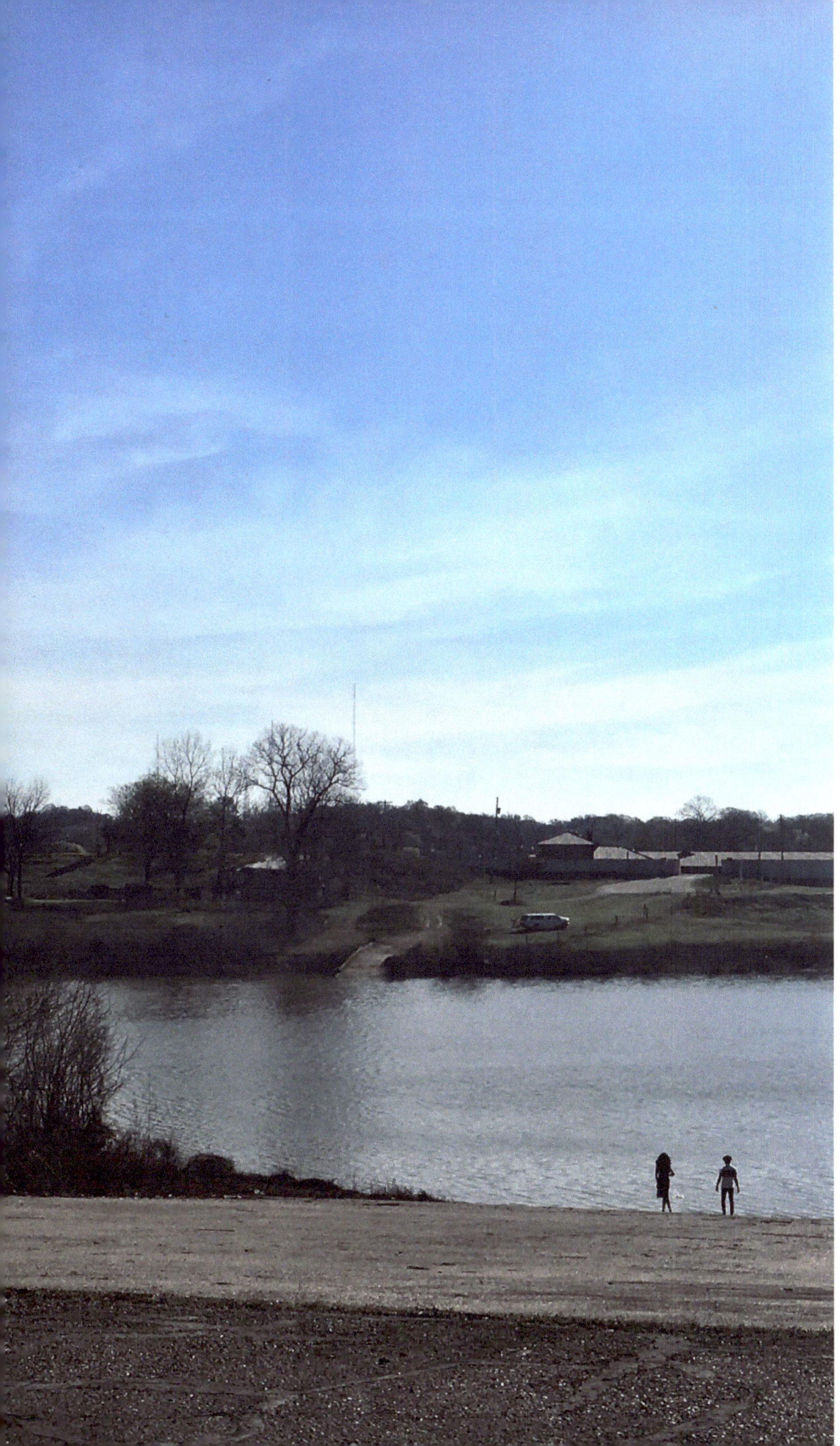

A *Huck Finn* Moment

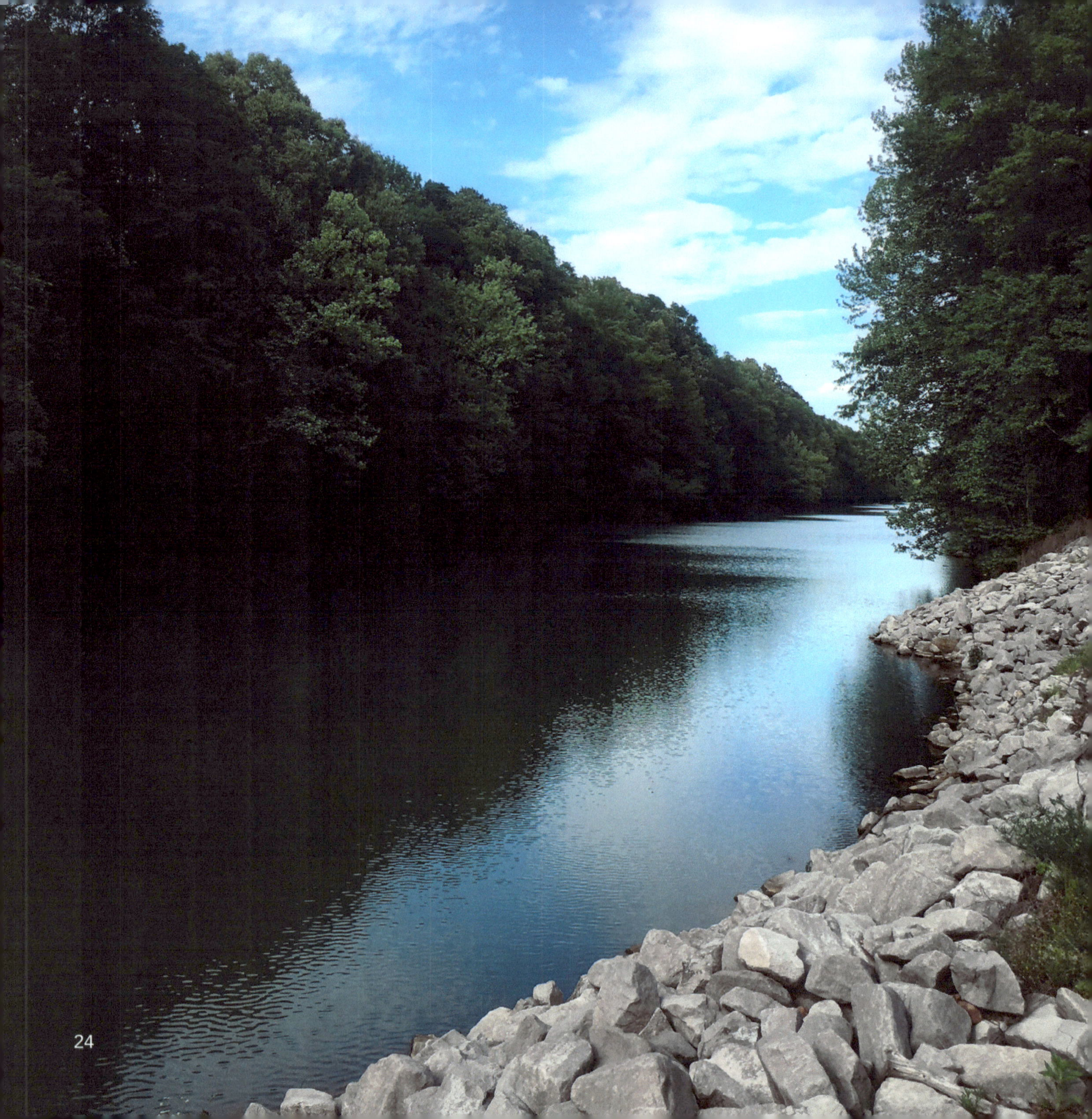

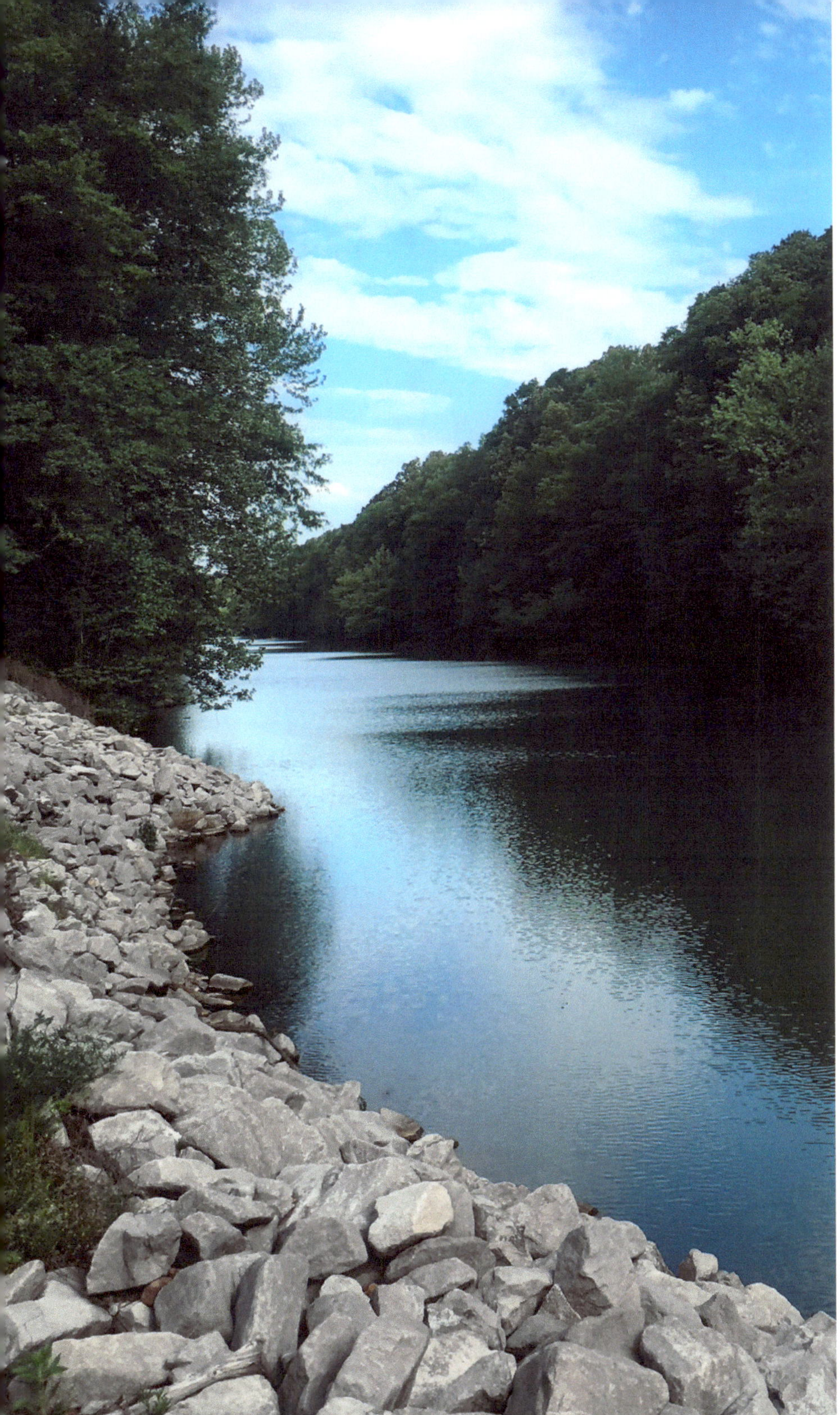

Calming Waters

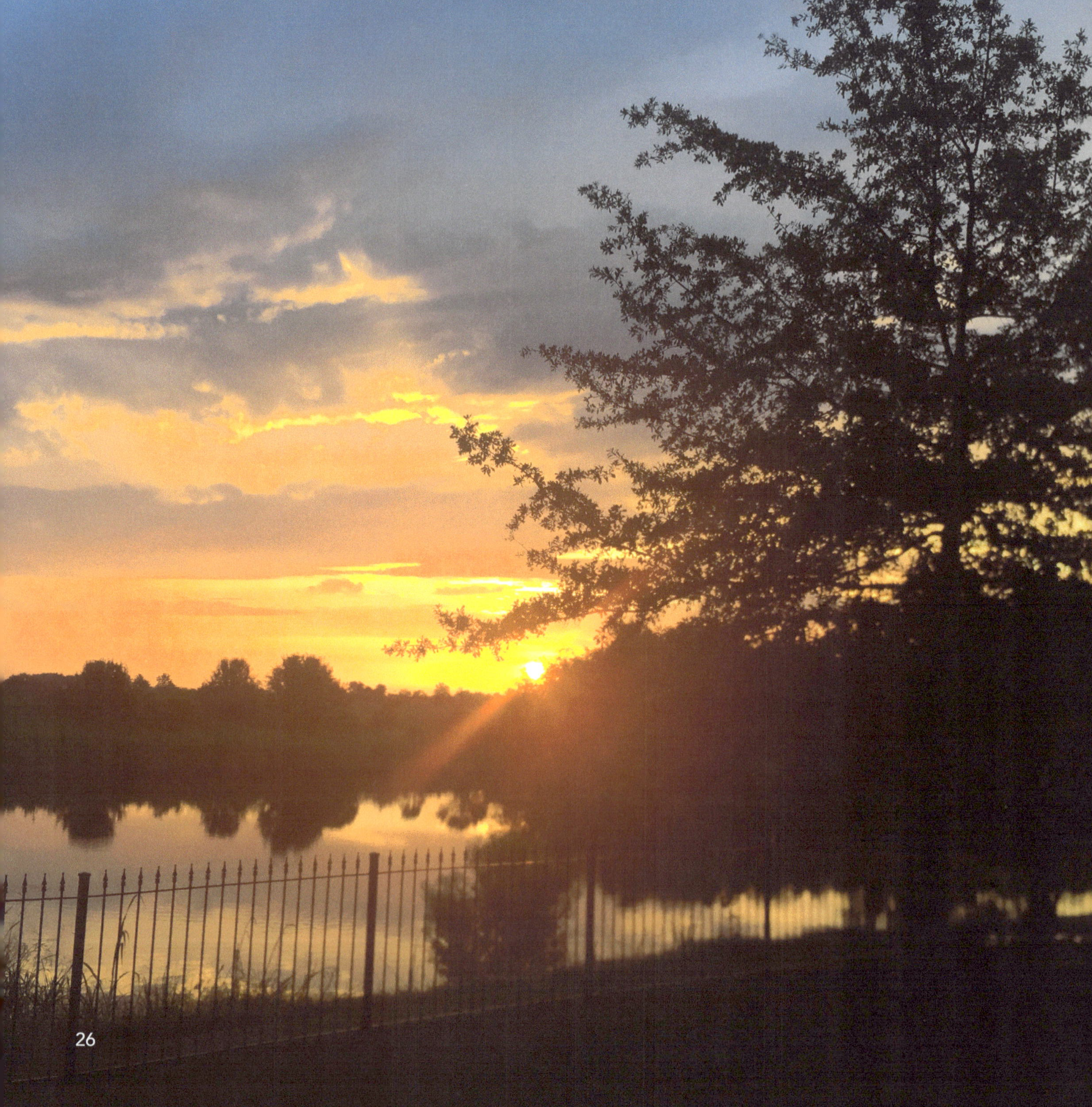

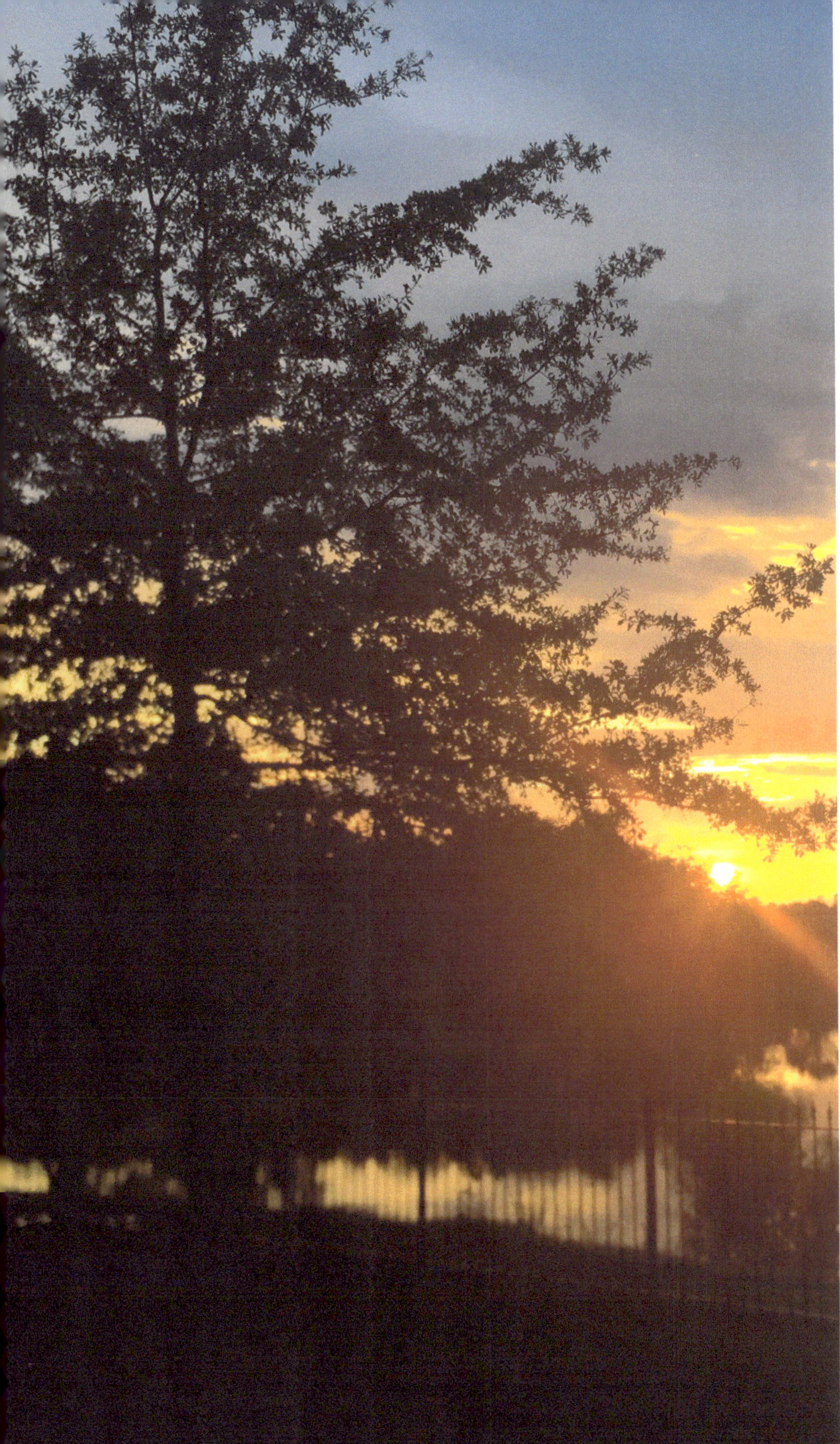

Creek Side Summer

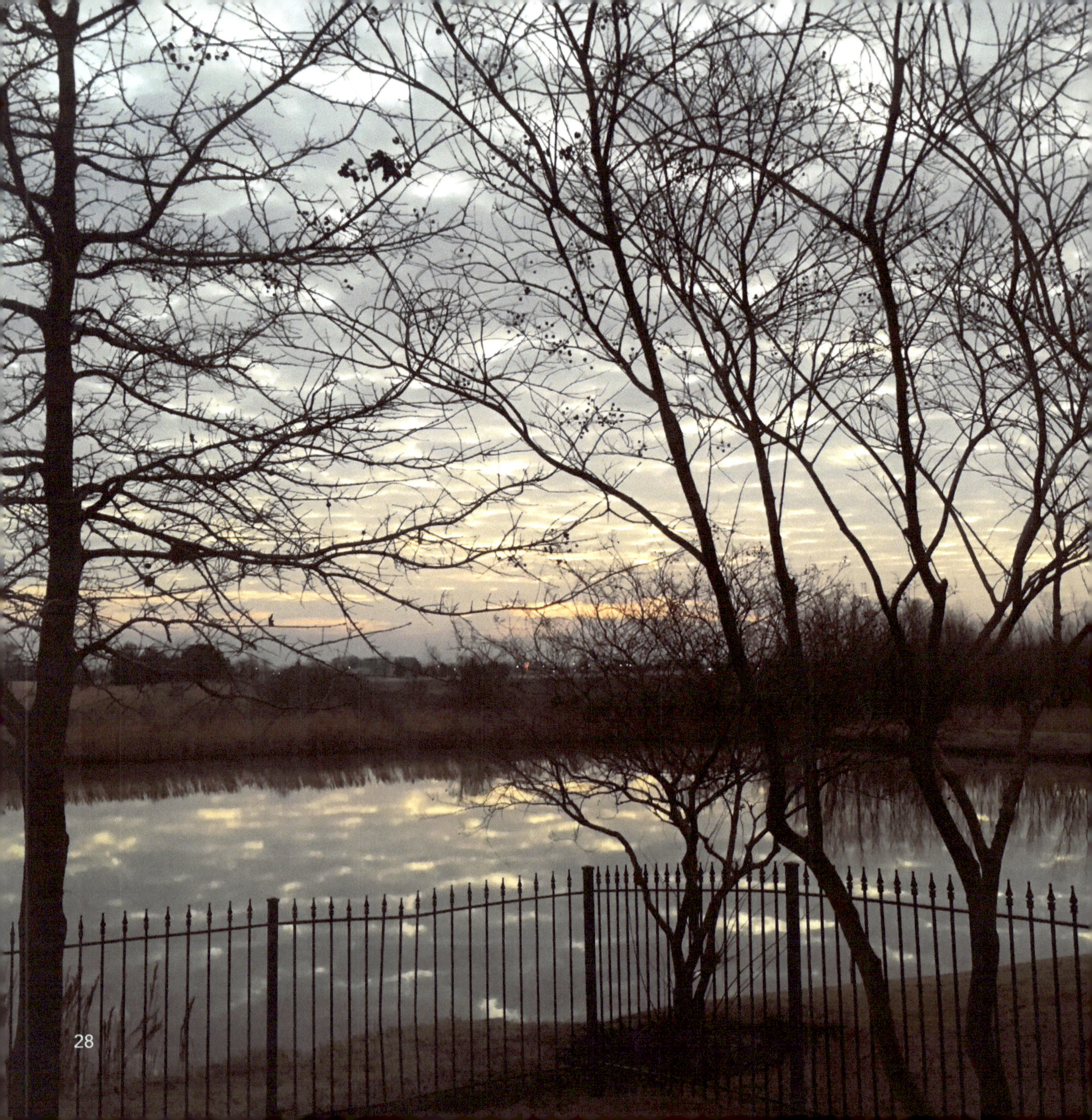

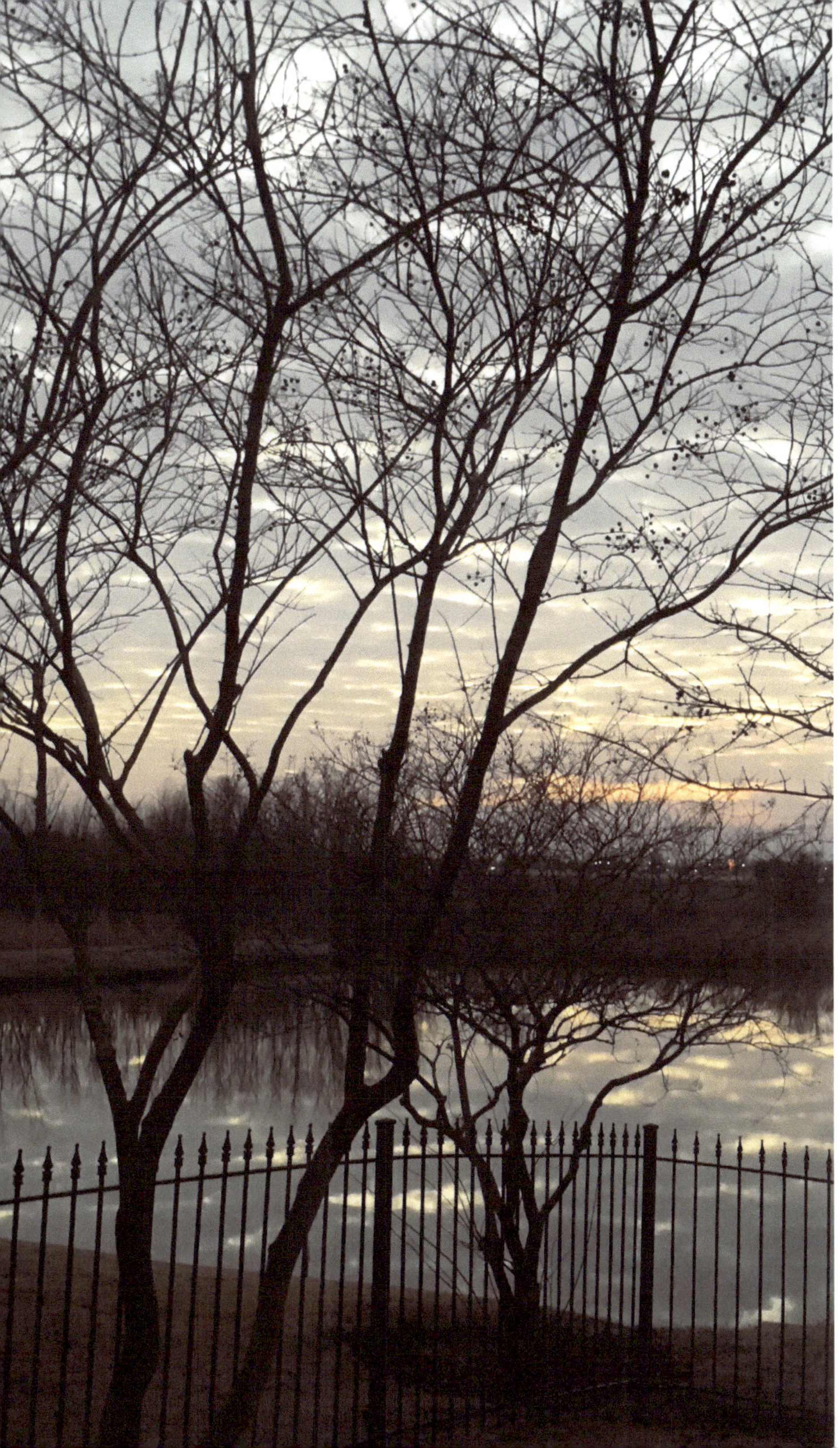

Creek Side Winter

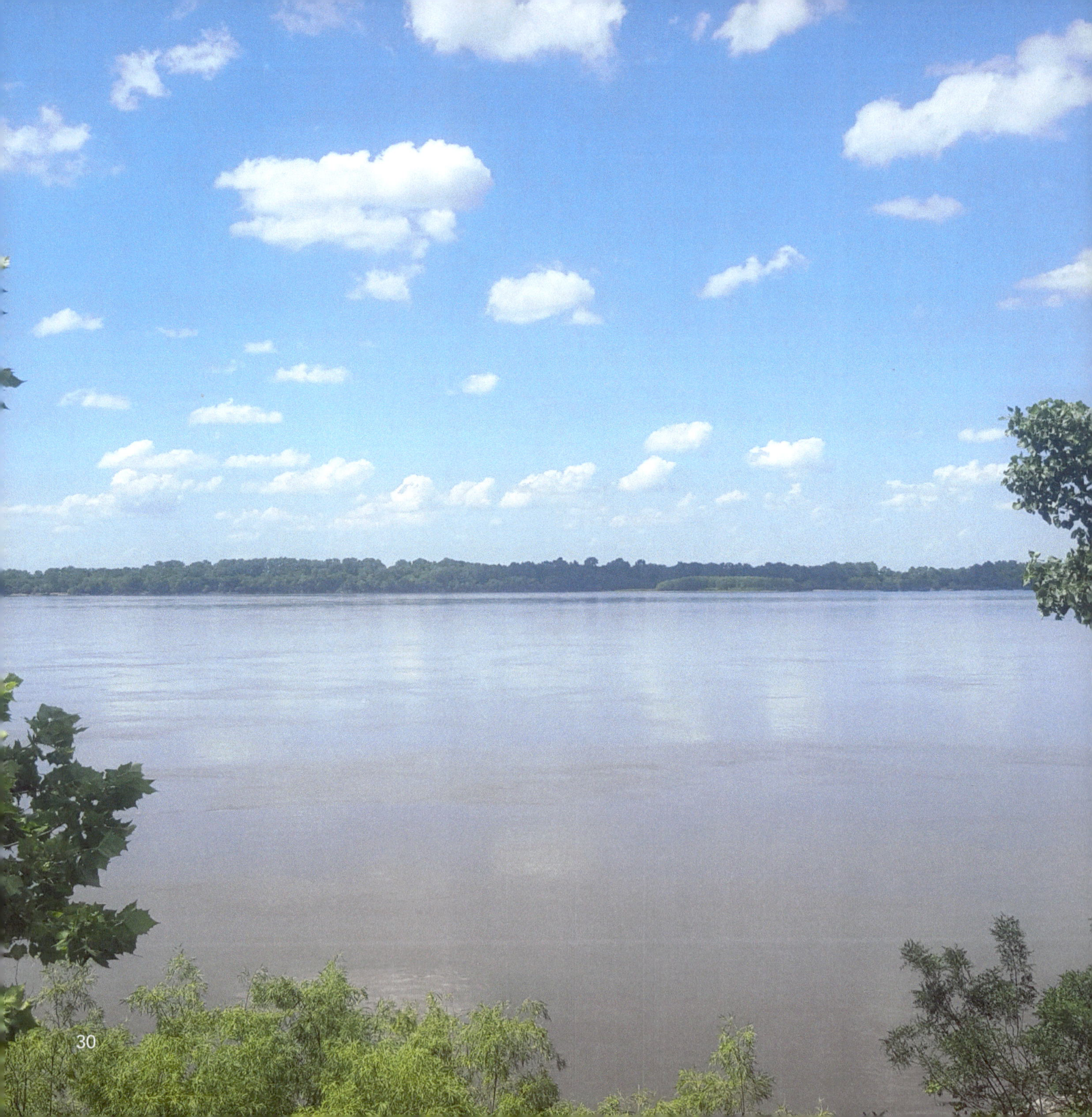

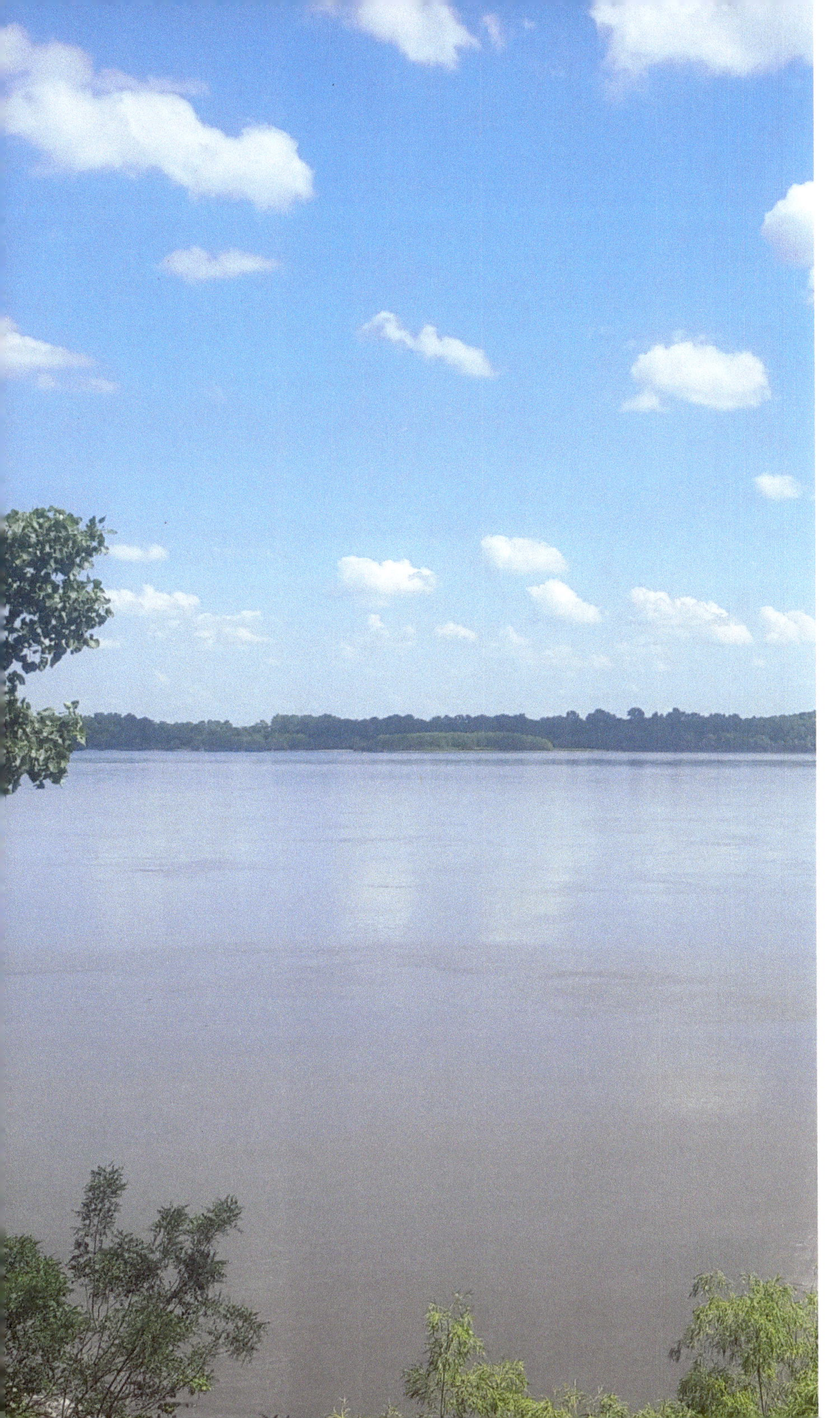

Muddy River Blue

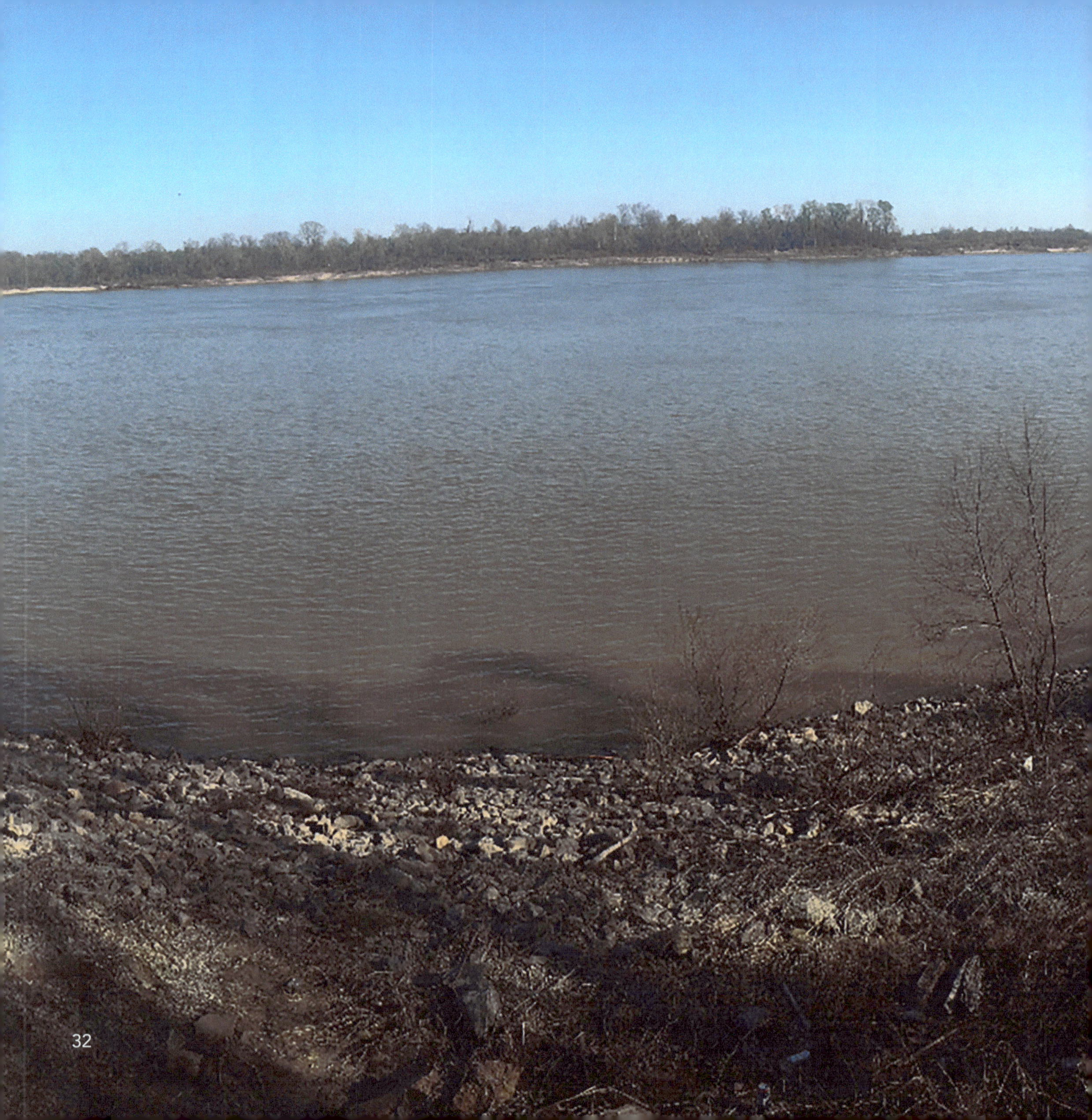

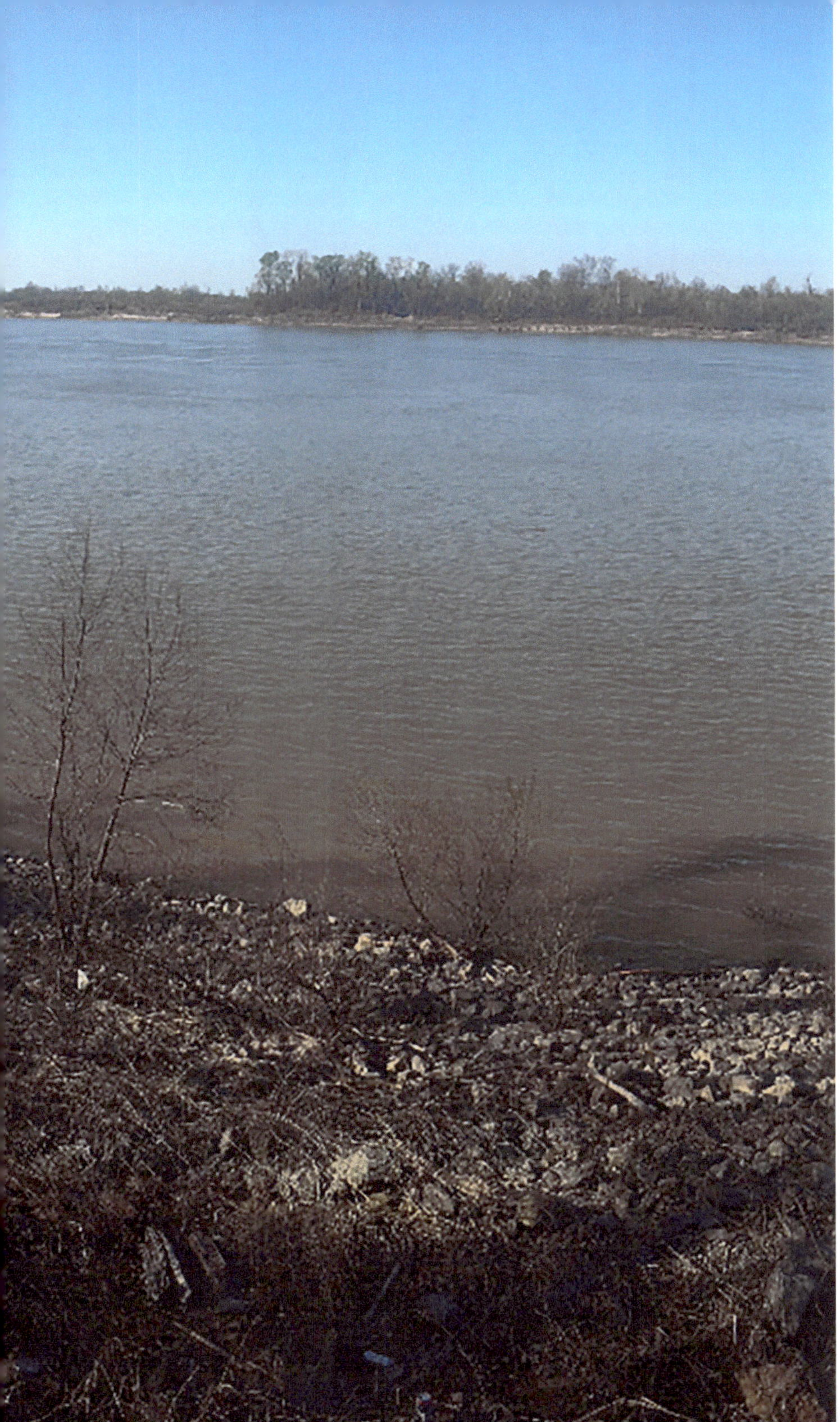

Brown River Banks

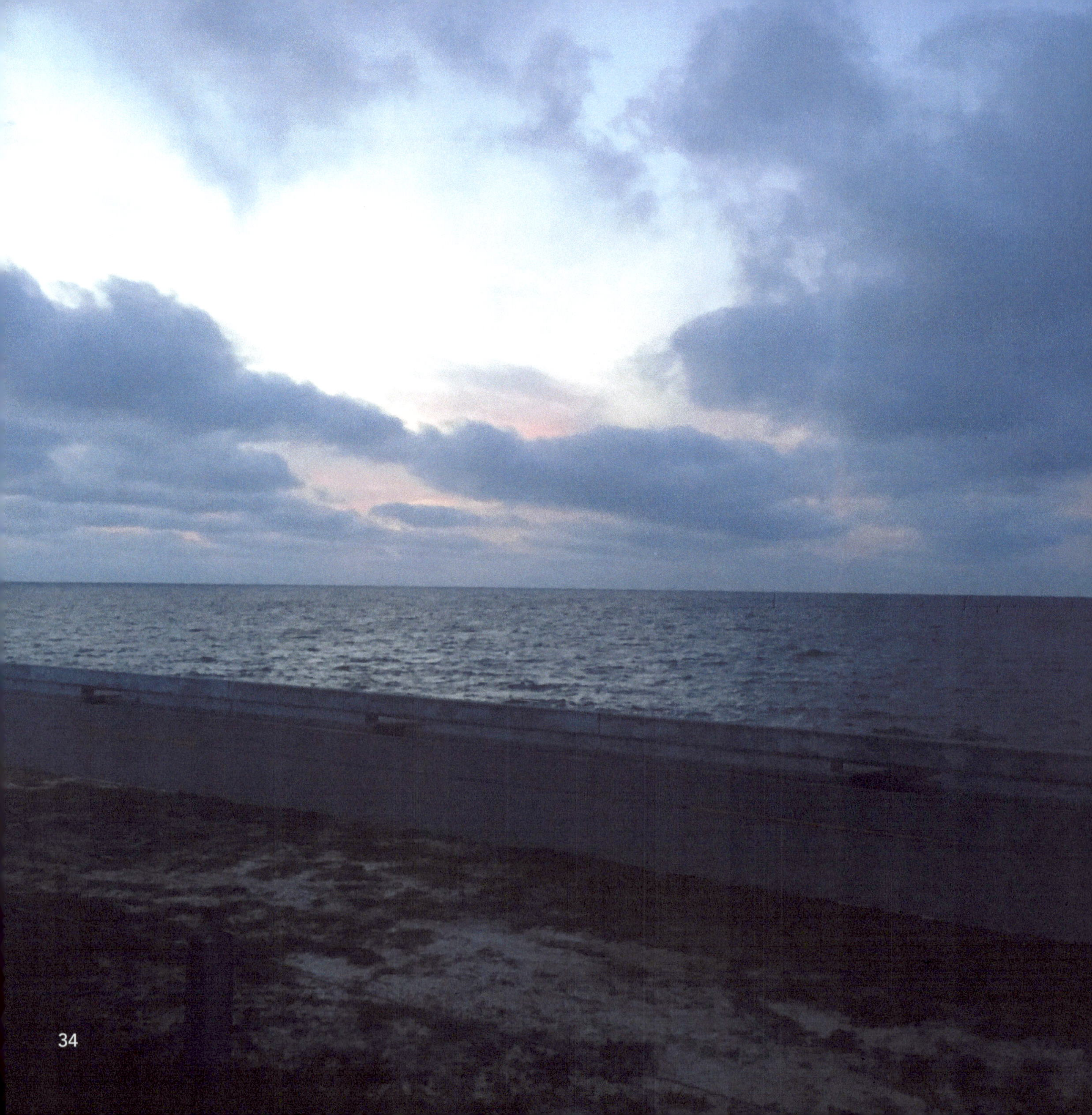

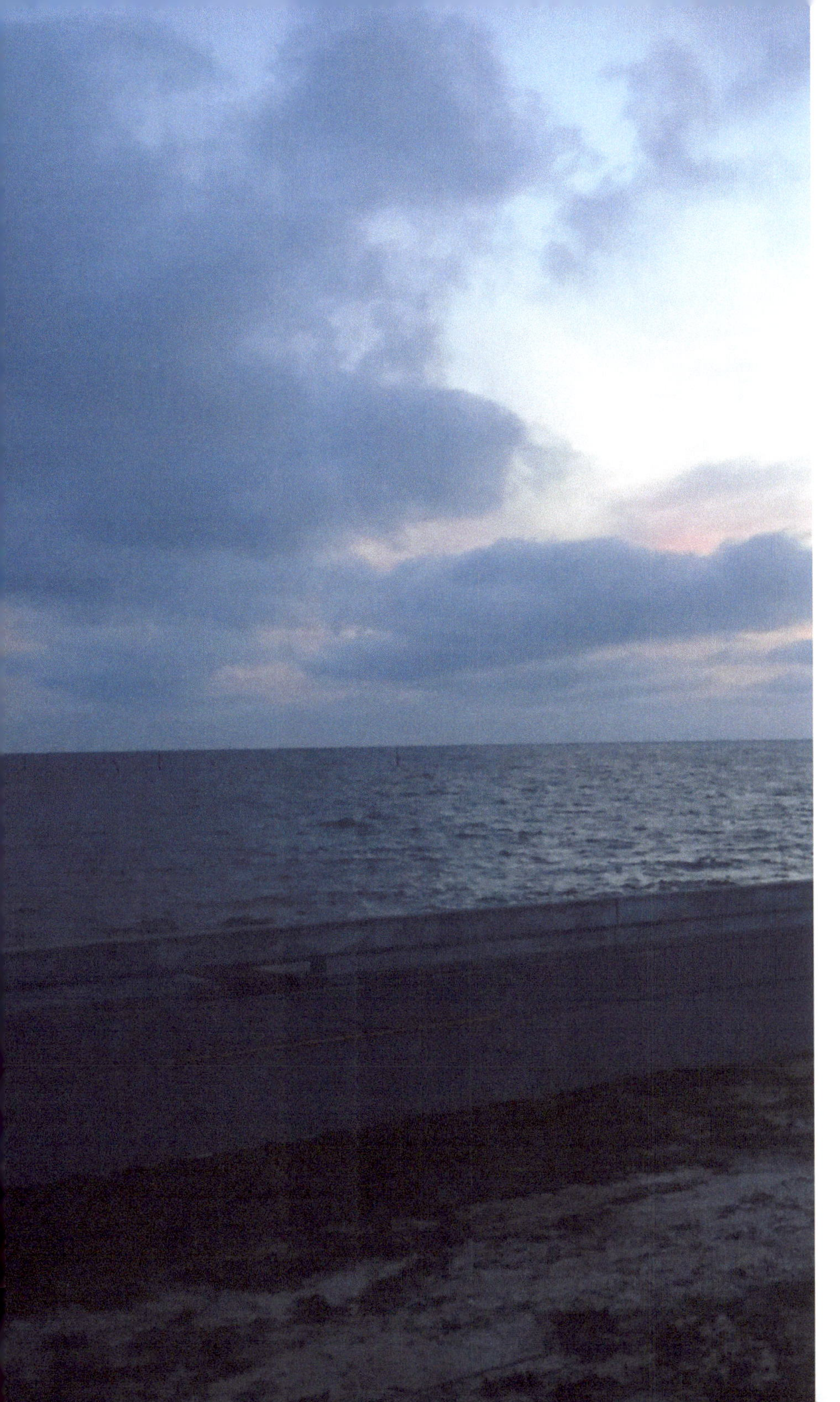

Mississippi Gulf Gray

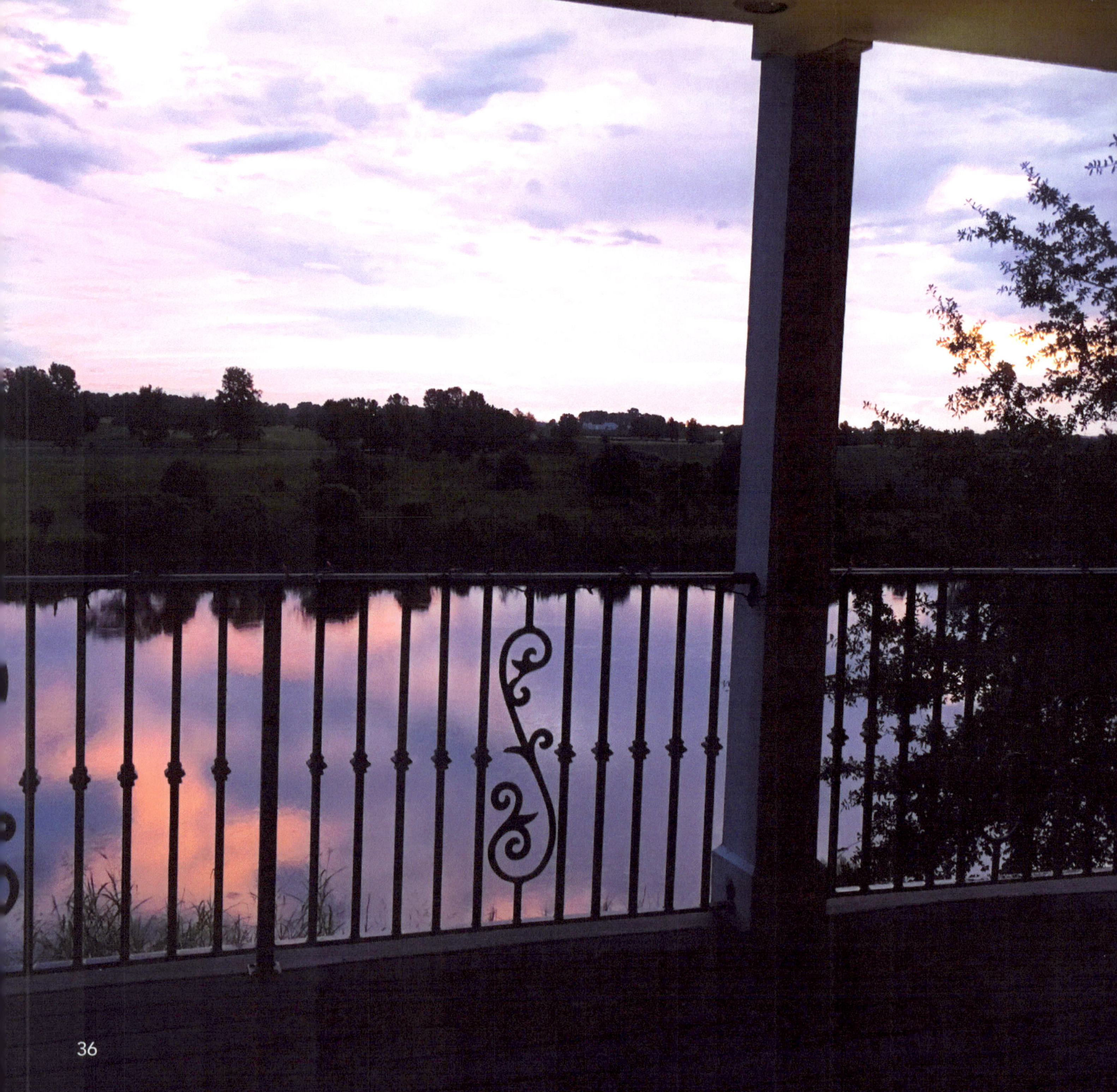

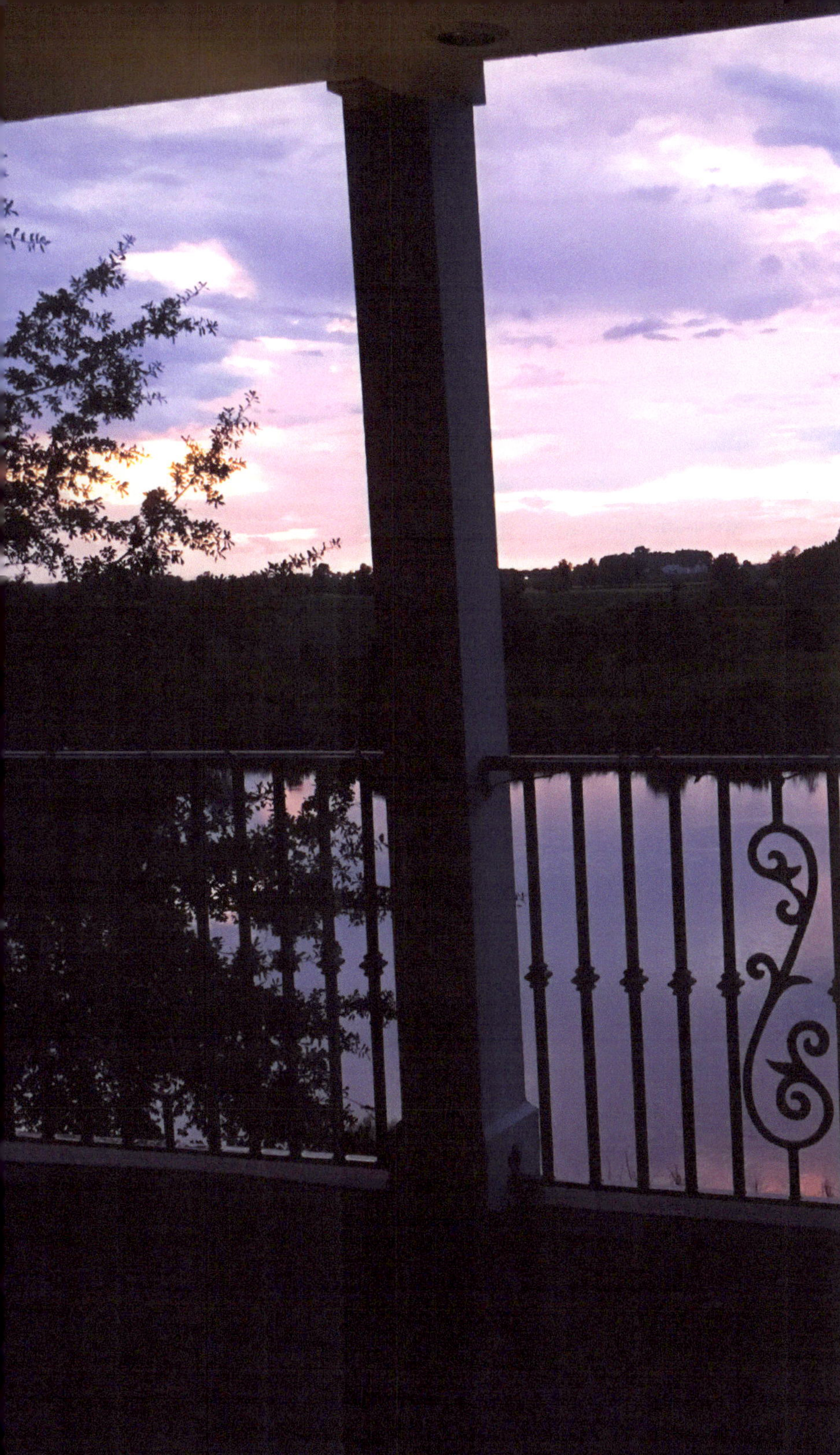

Violet Not Violence

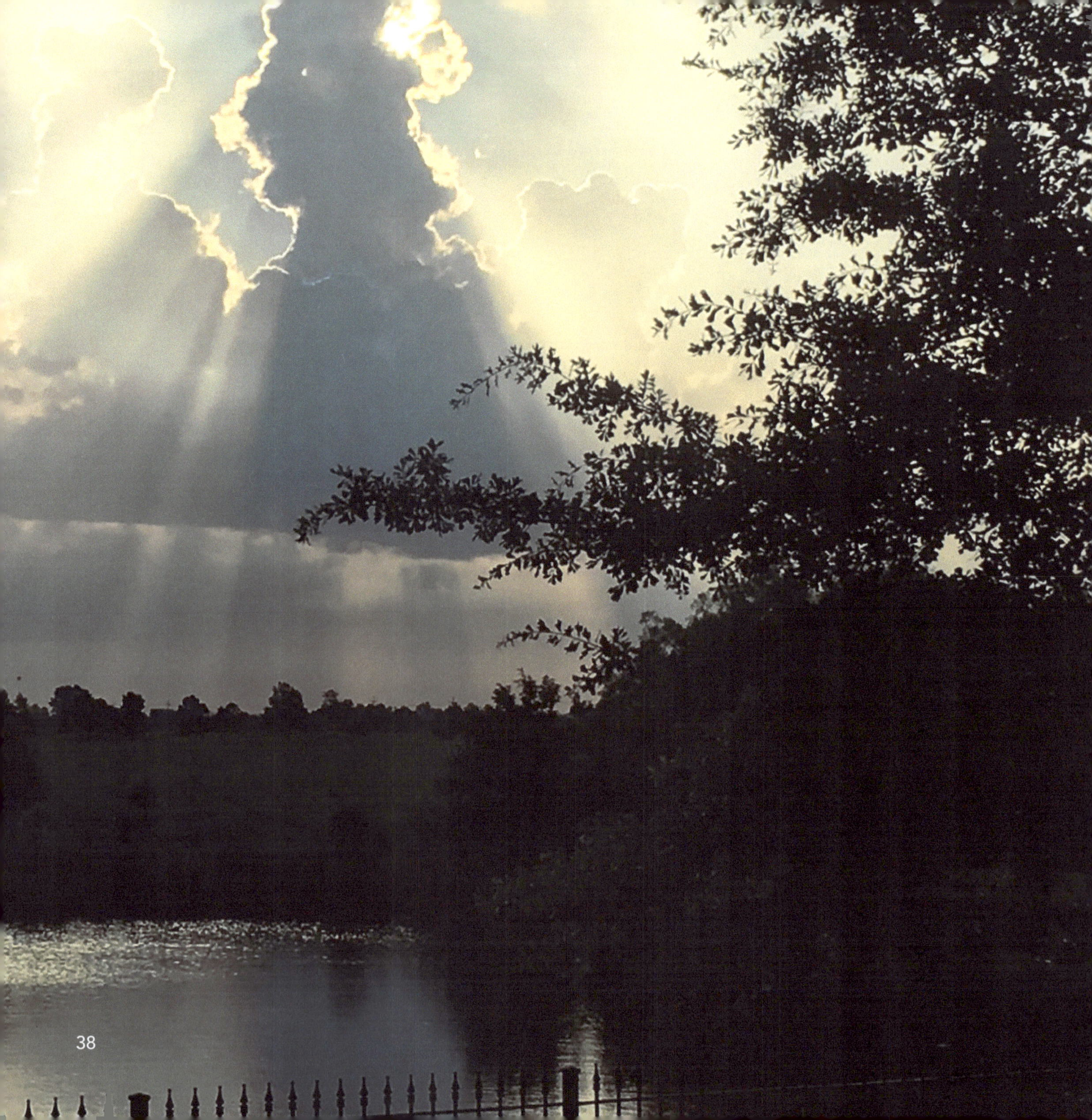

2

DELTA SKIES

Look up to the skies for inspiration. The skies are available. They do not need to be sunny, clear and blue for me to be inspired. I enjoy the ever changing view. I encourage you to enjoy them too.

The truth is that reputation has its history. The civil dissension that took place over the past few hundred years has not had an impact on these beautiful skies. Behold these beautiful skies, enjoy, reflect and find peace.

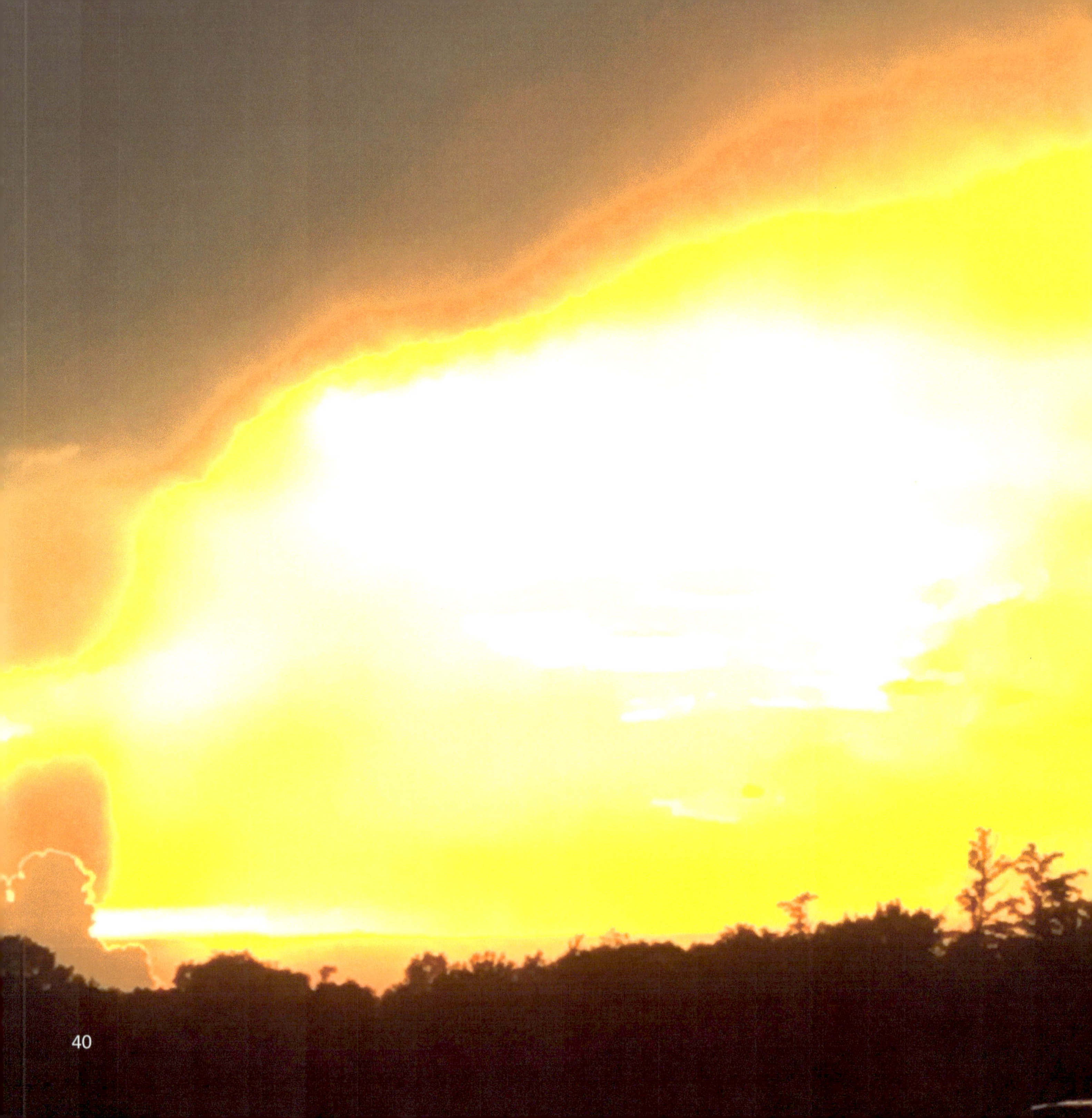

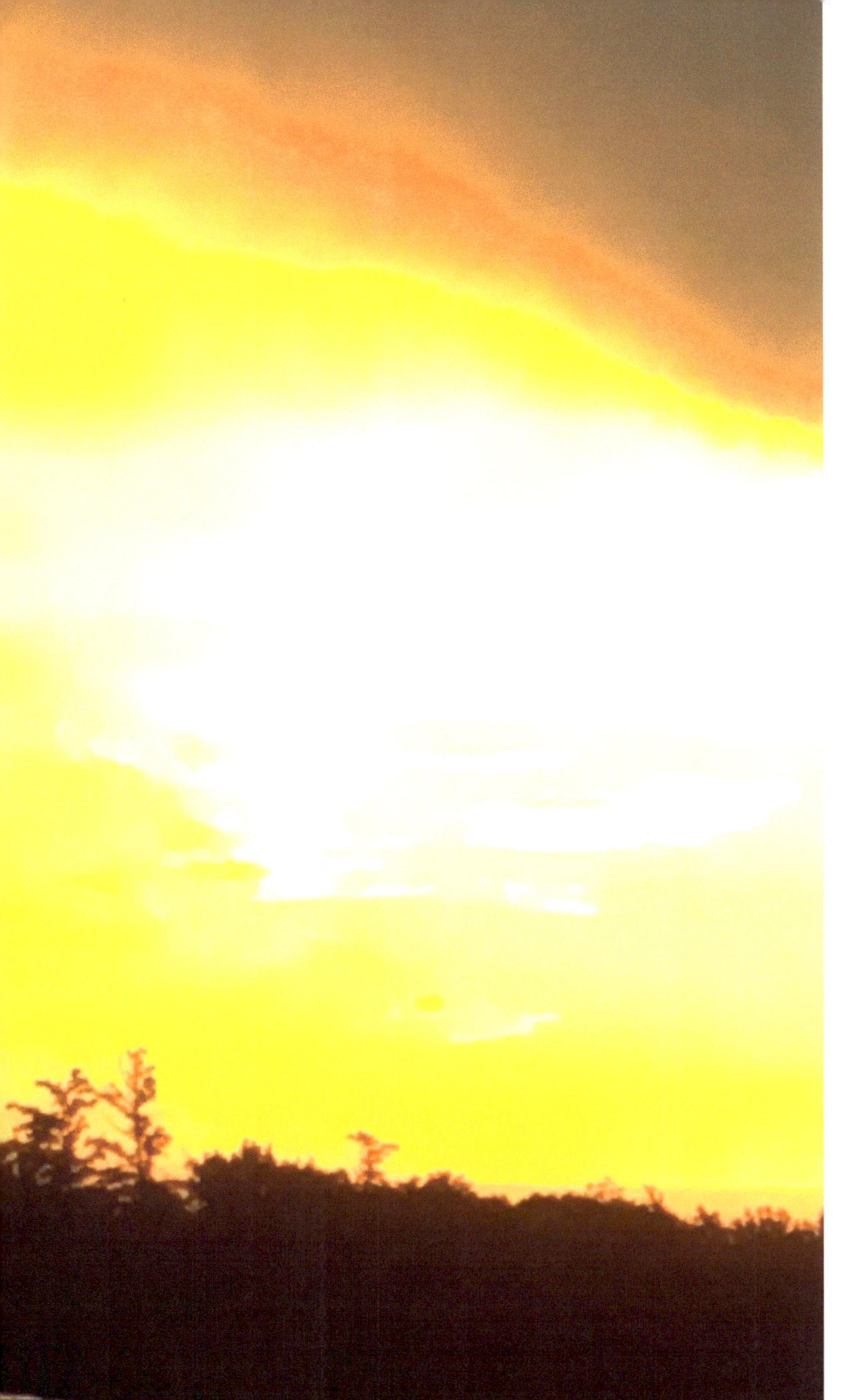

24k Pure Gold

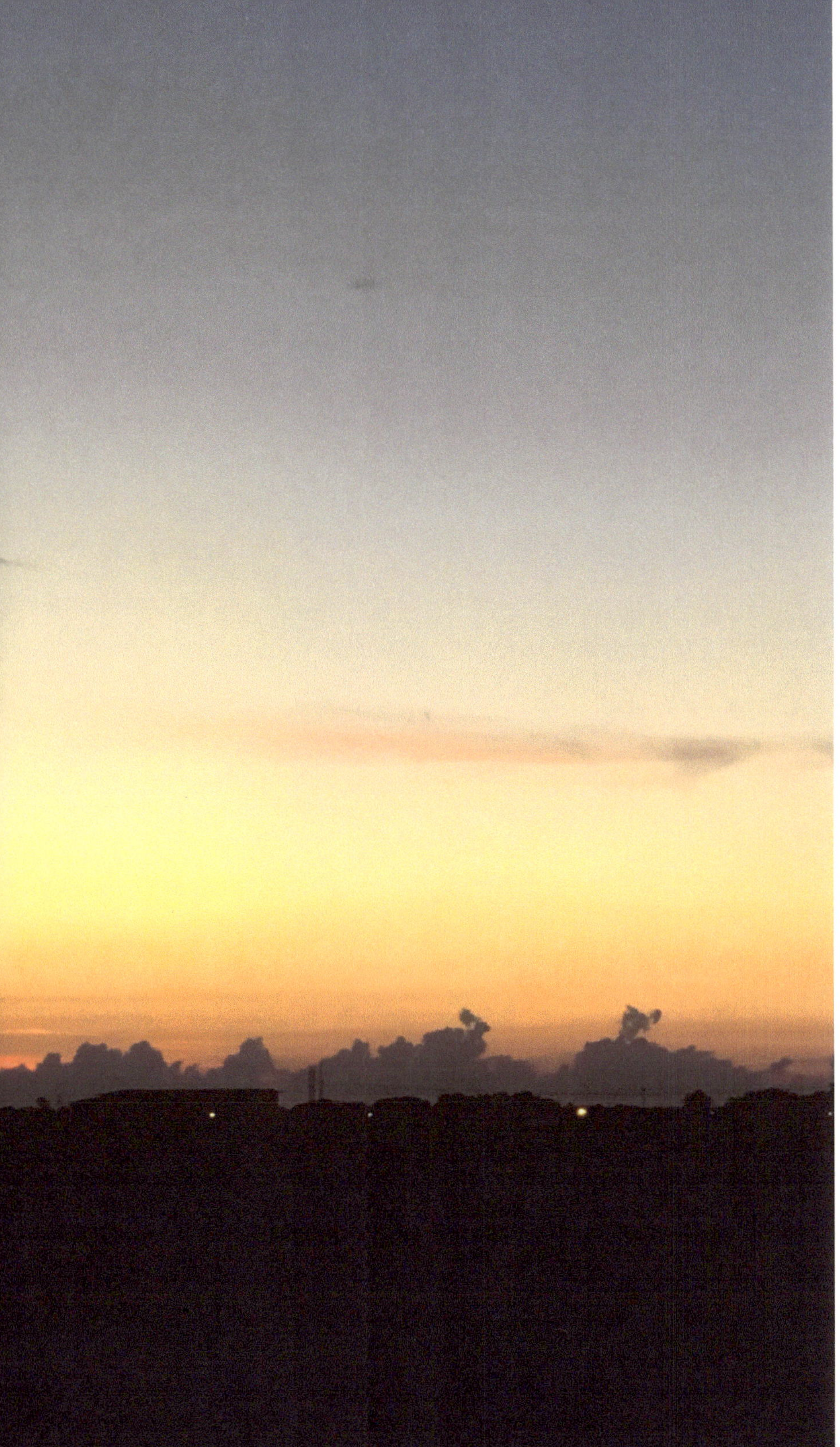

"Sippi" Silhouette

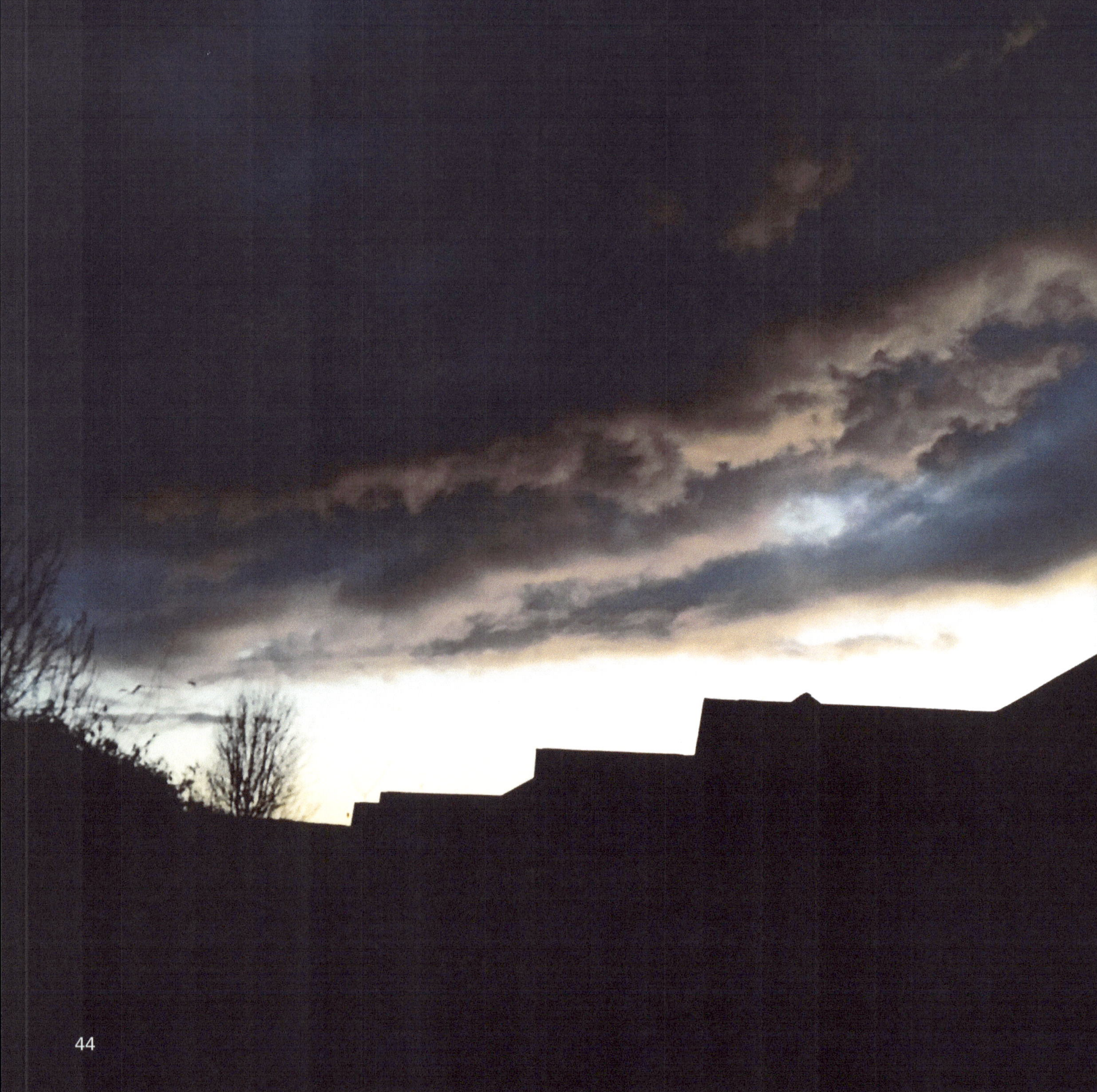

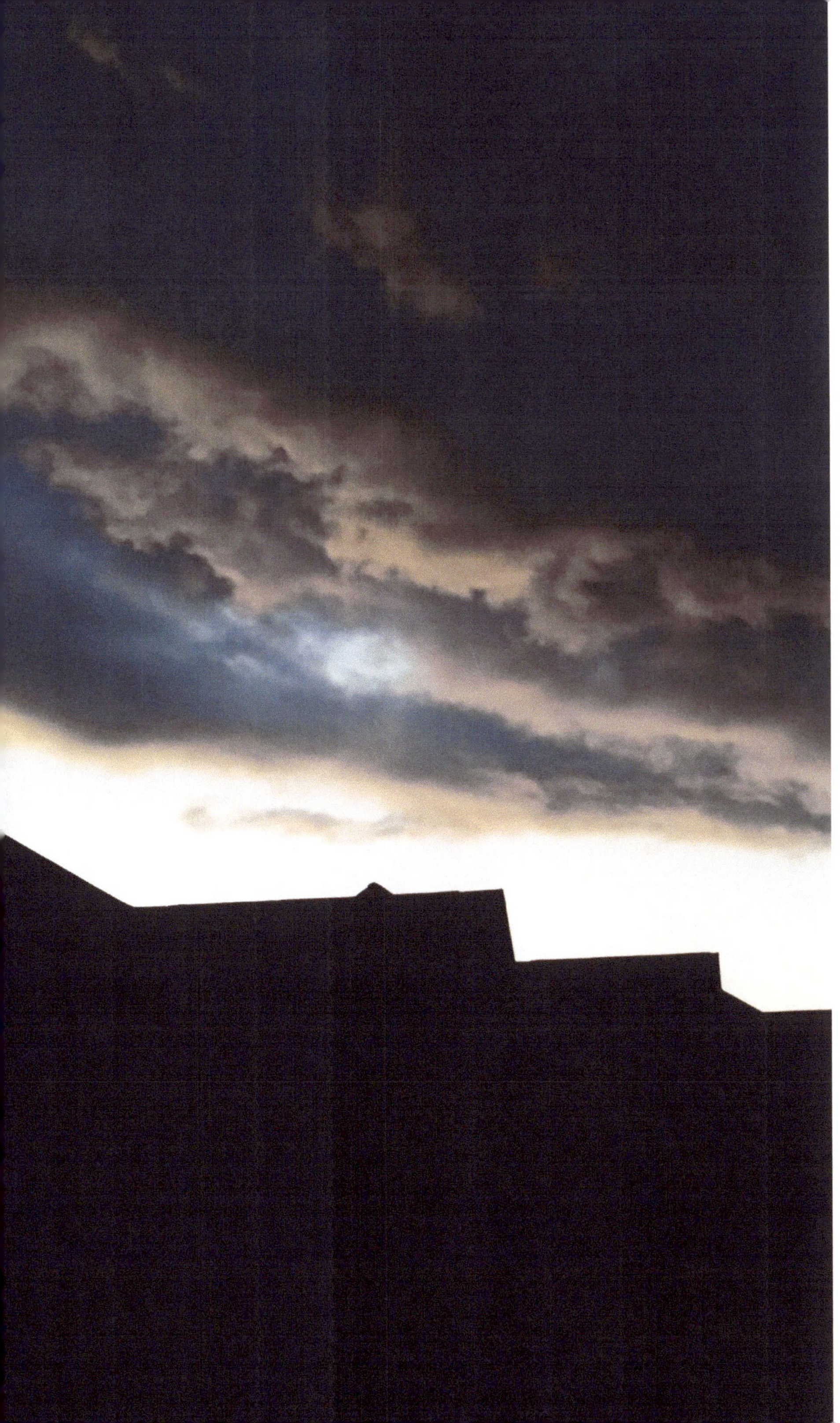

Smoke Stack Howlin

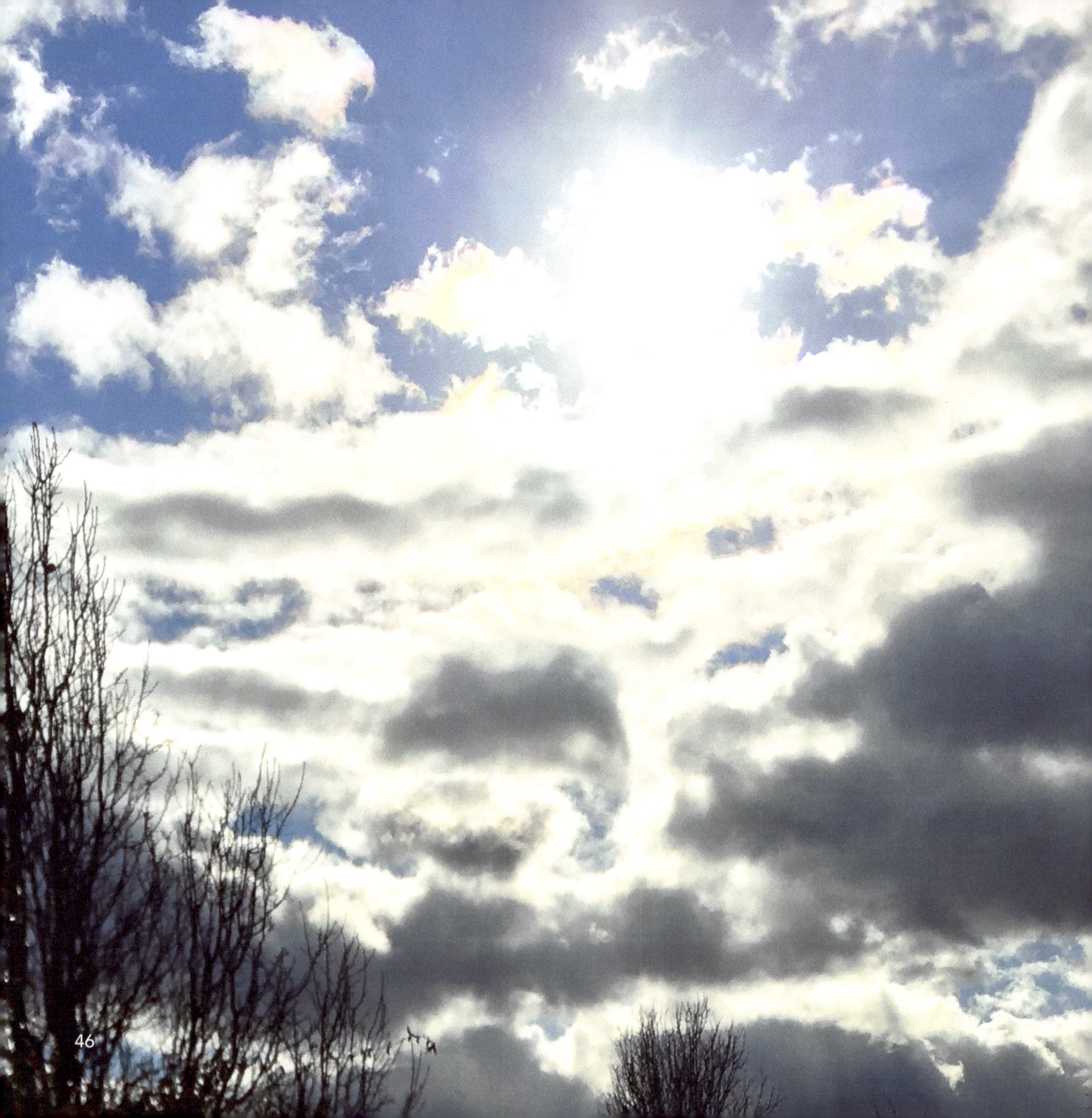

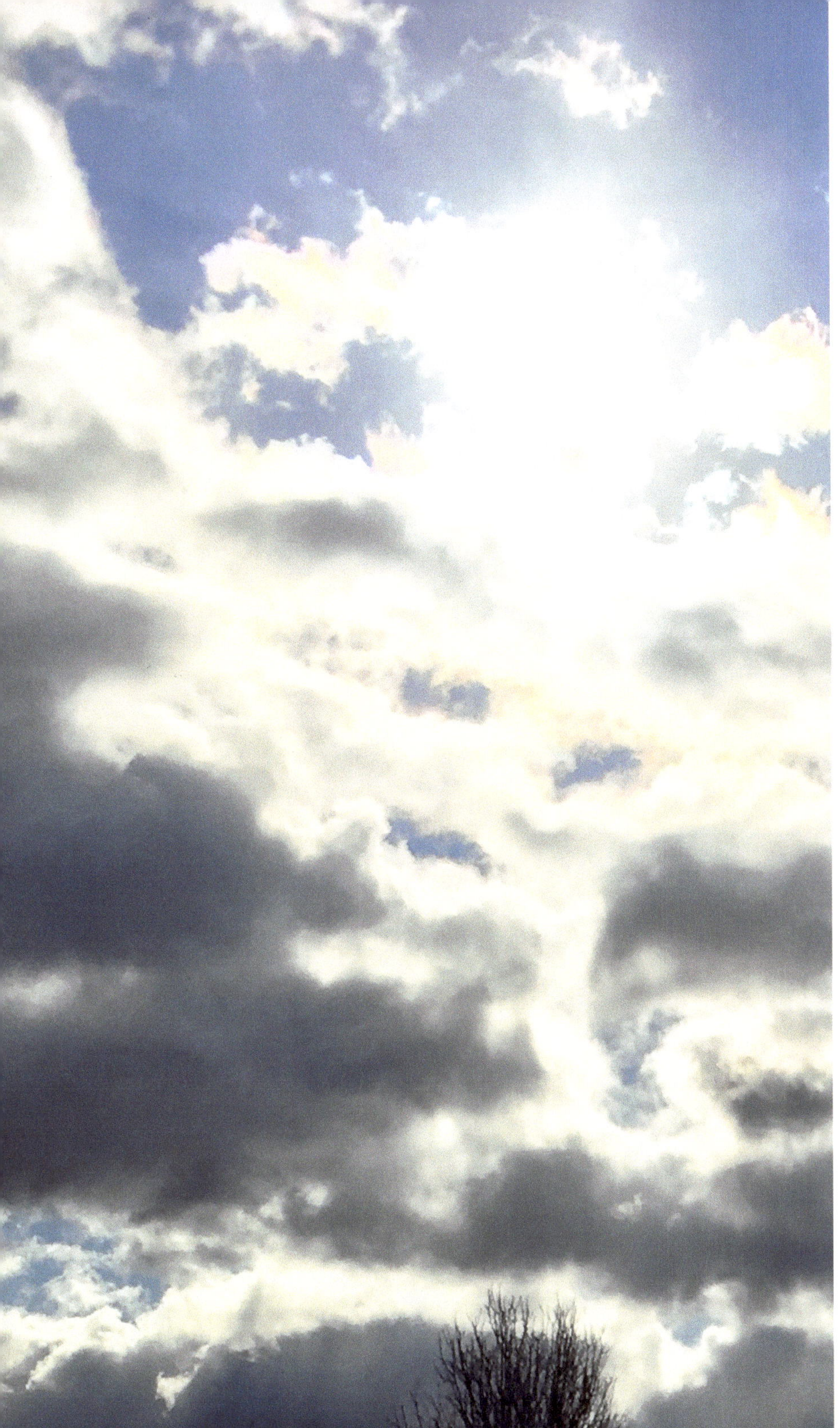

Breakthru

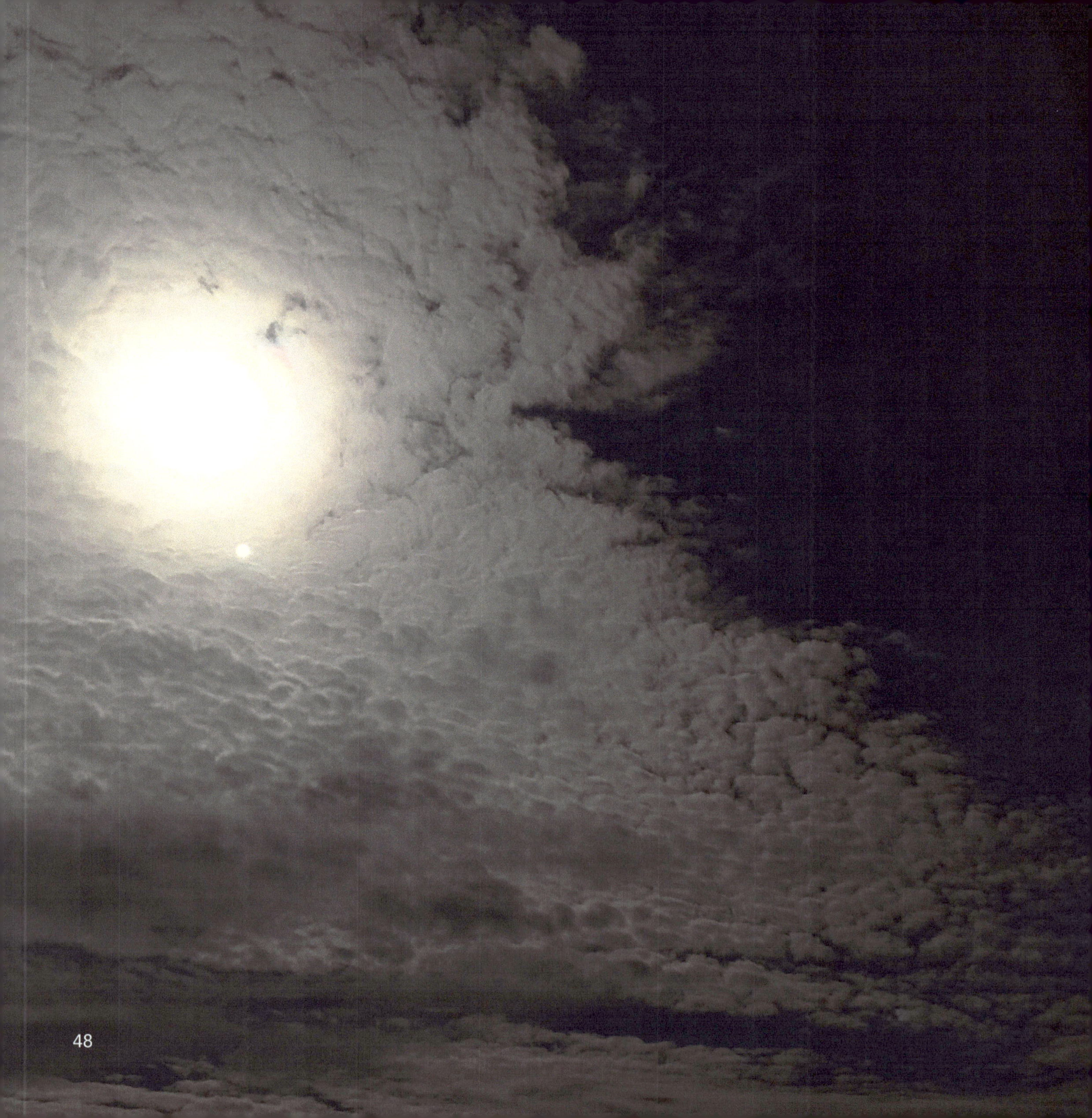

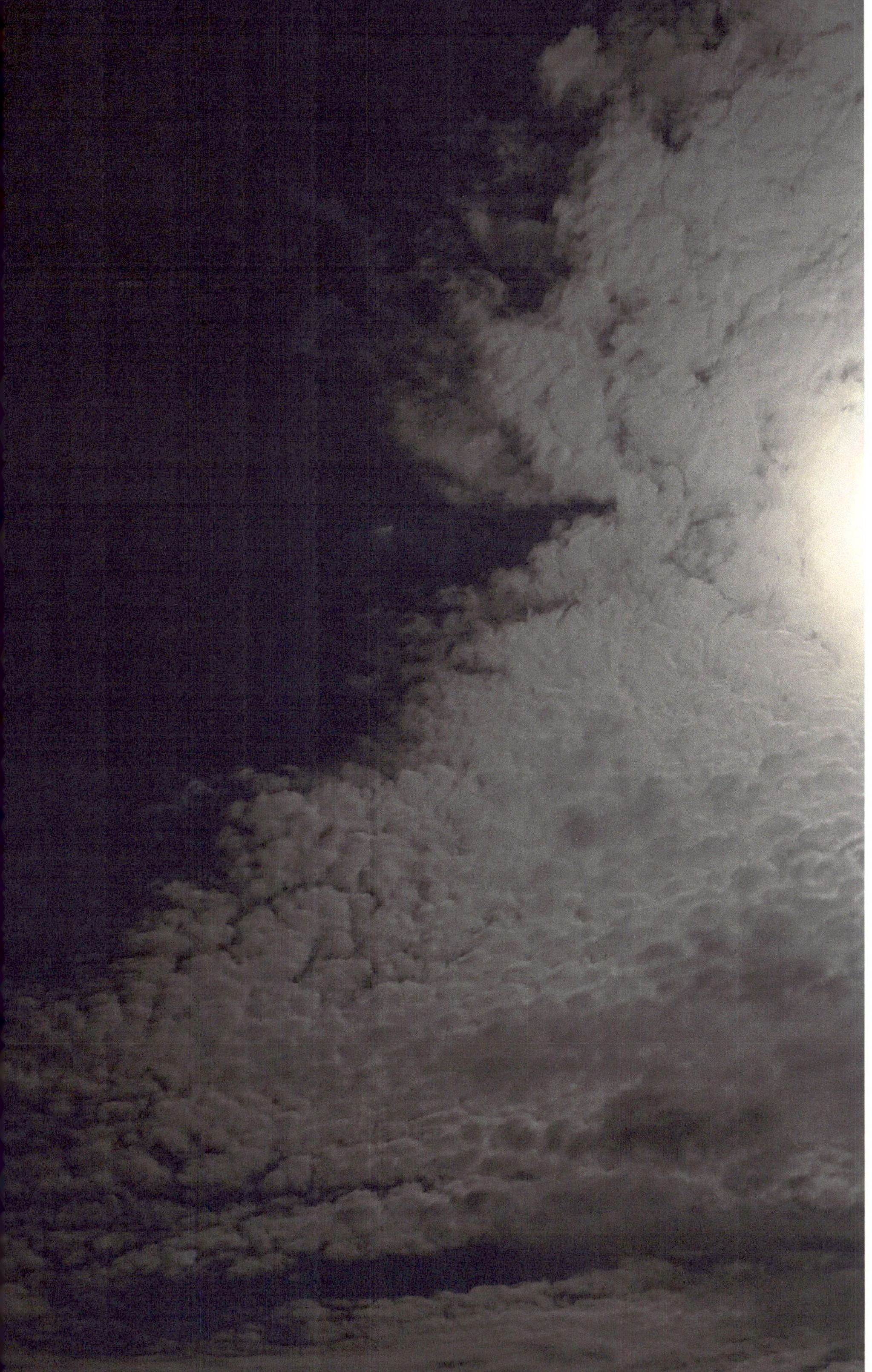

Glow

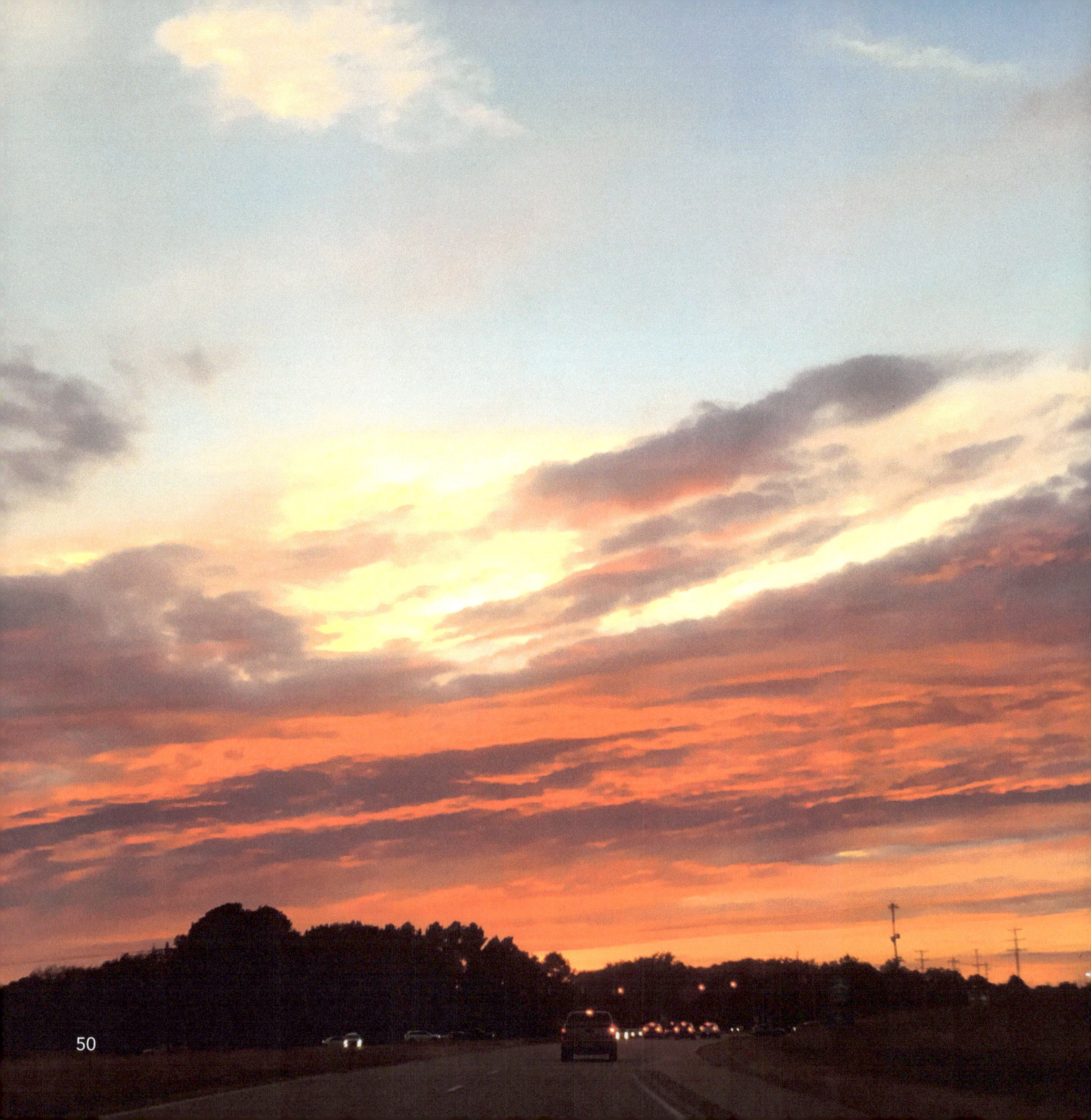

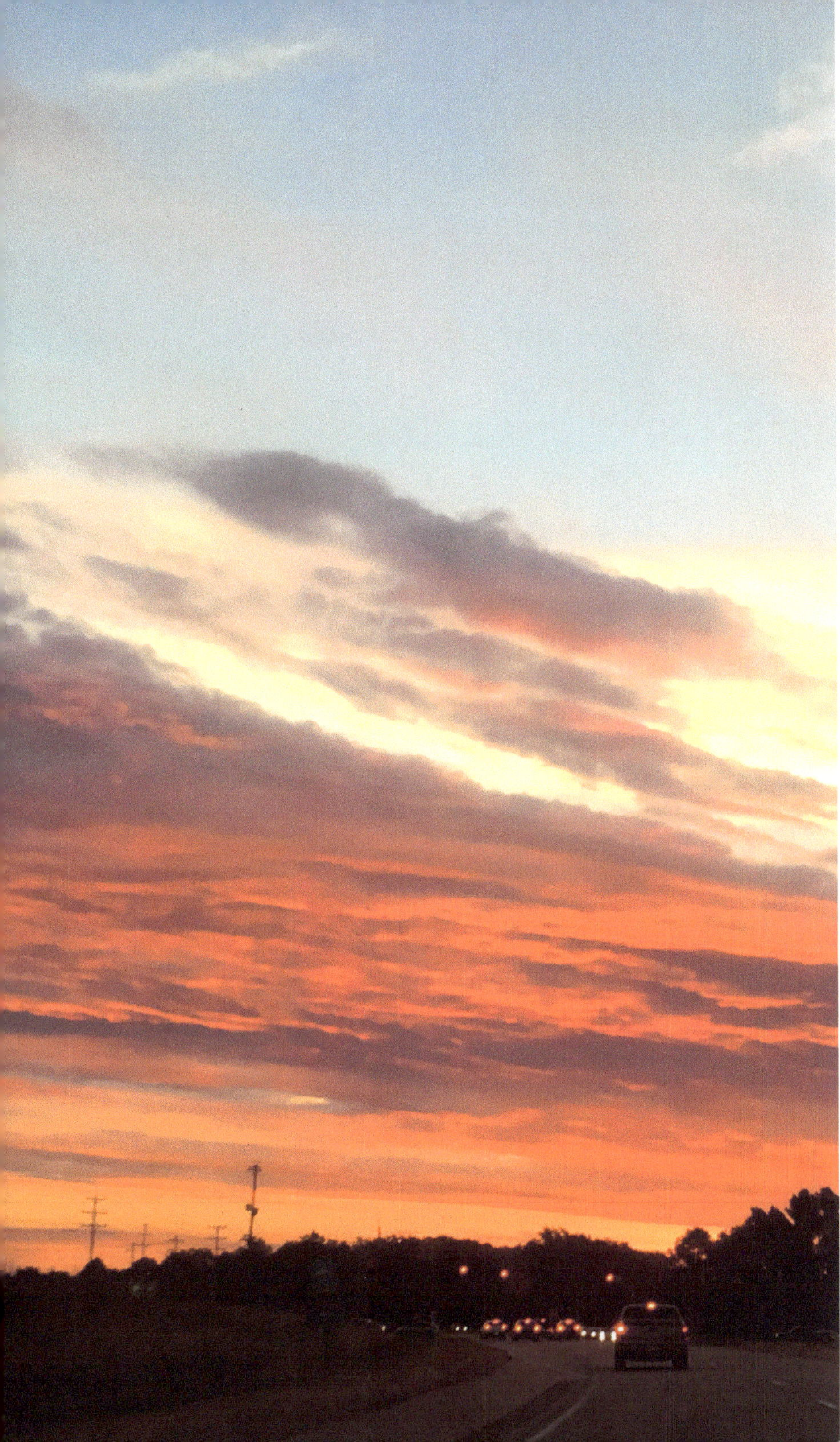

Brake Light Sunset

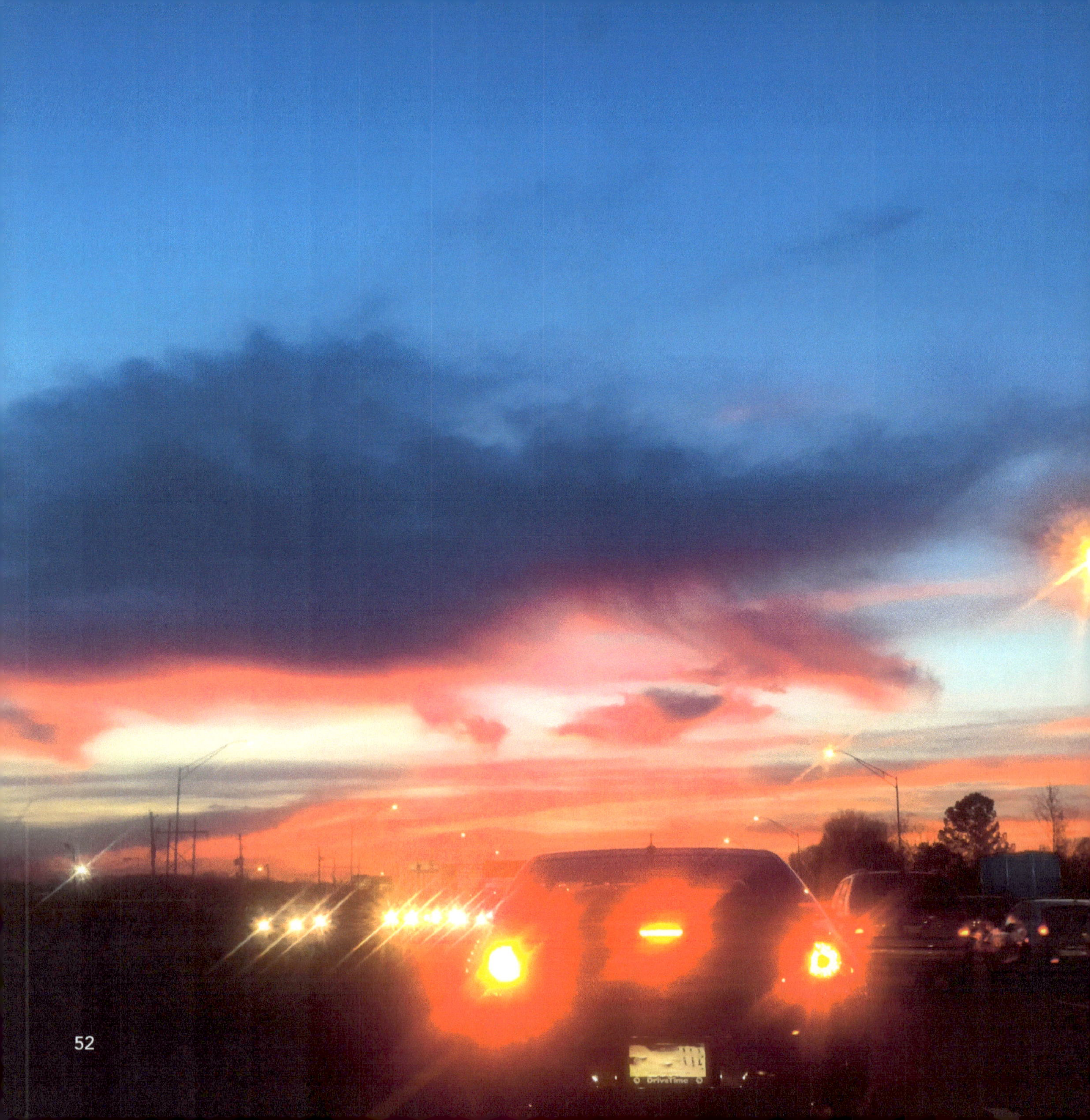
DriveTime

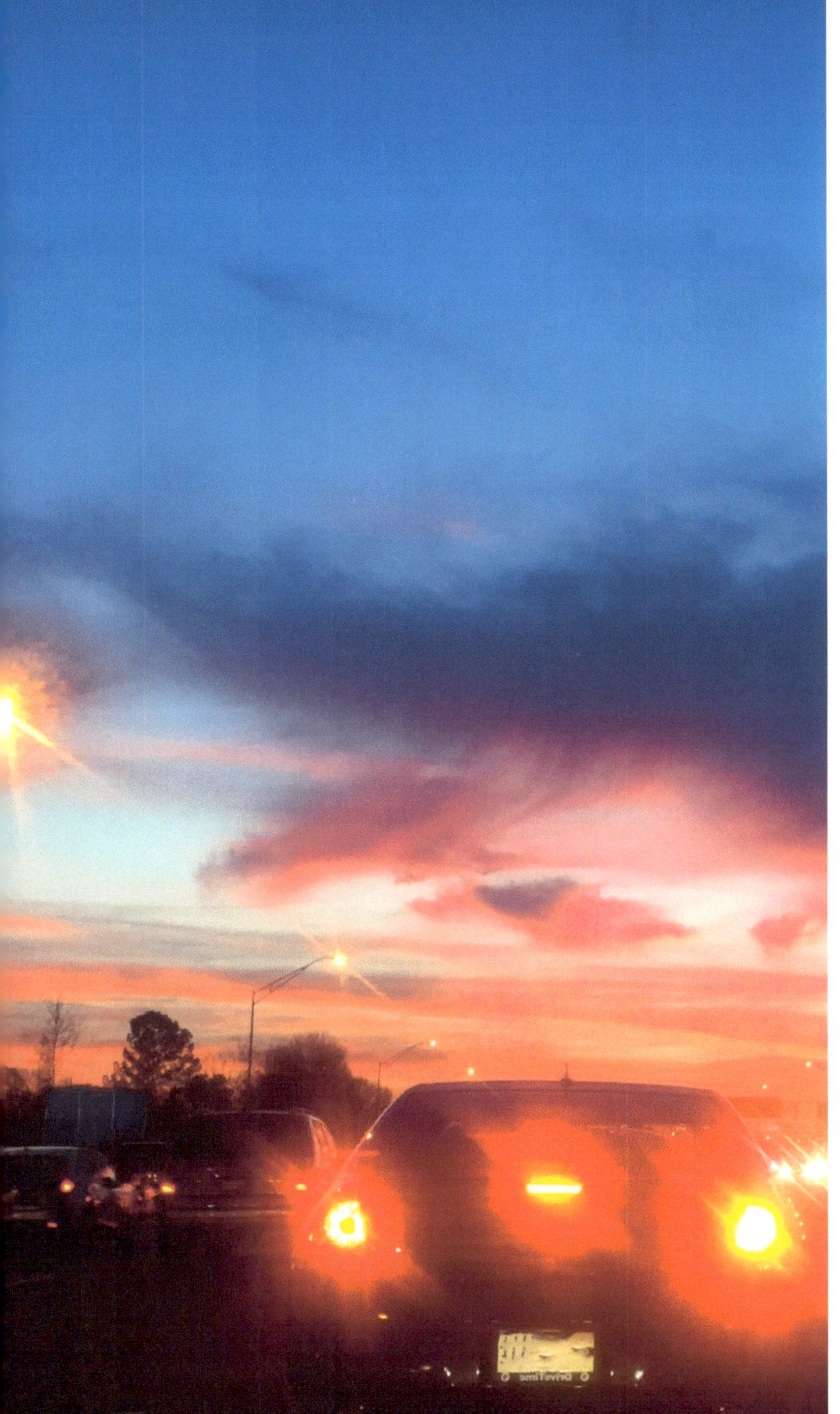

Blazzin Blue Commute

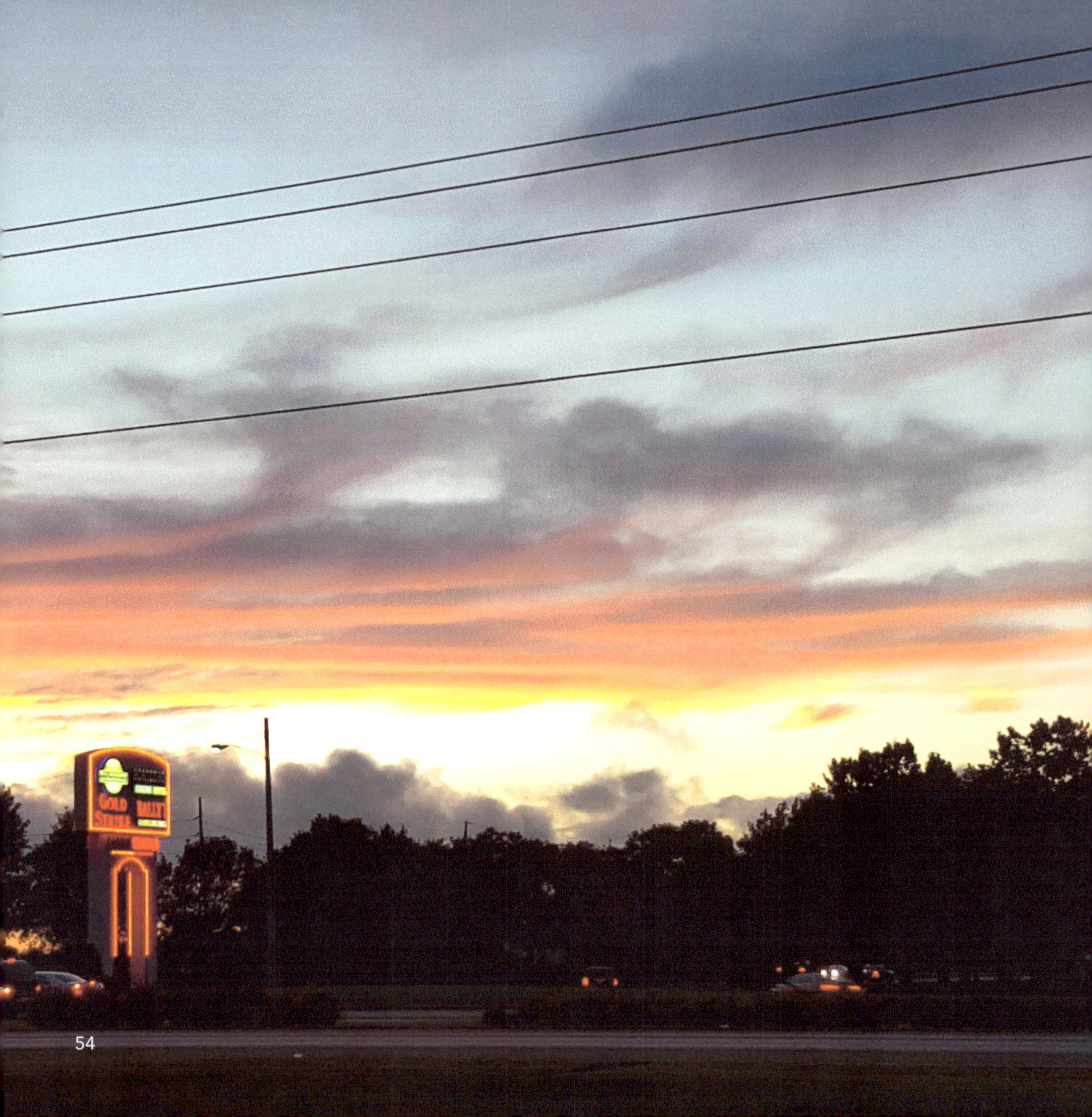
GOLD
STRIKE

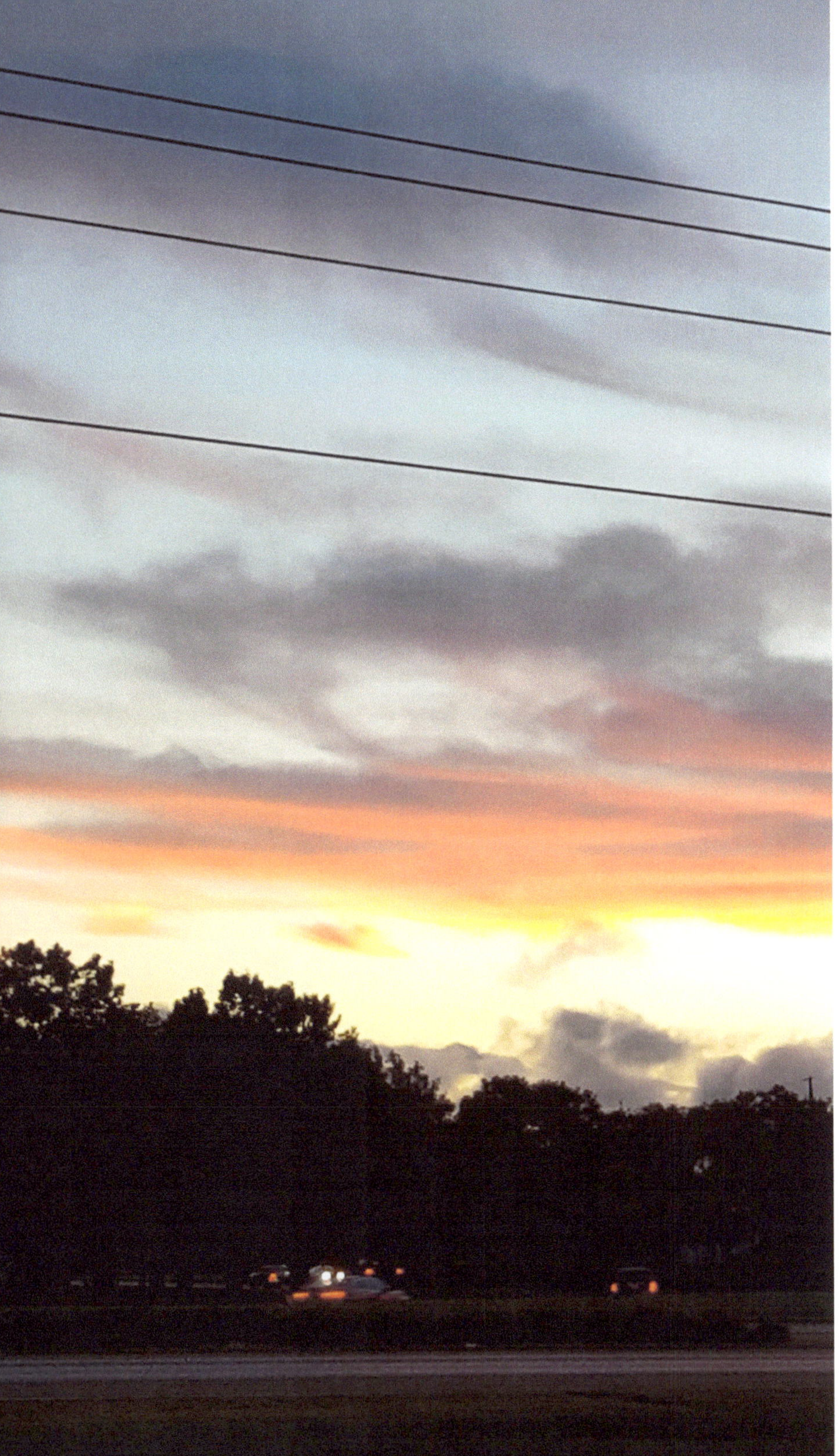

Neon Natural

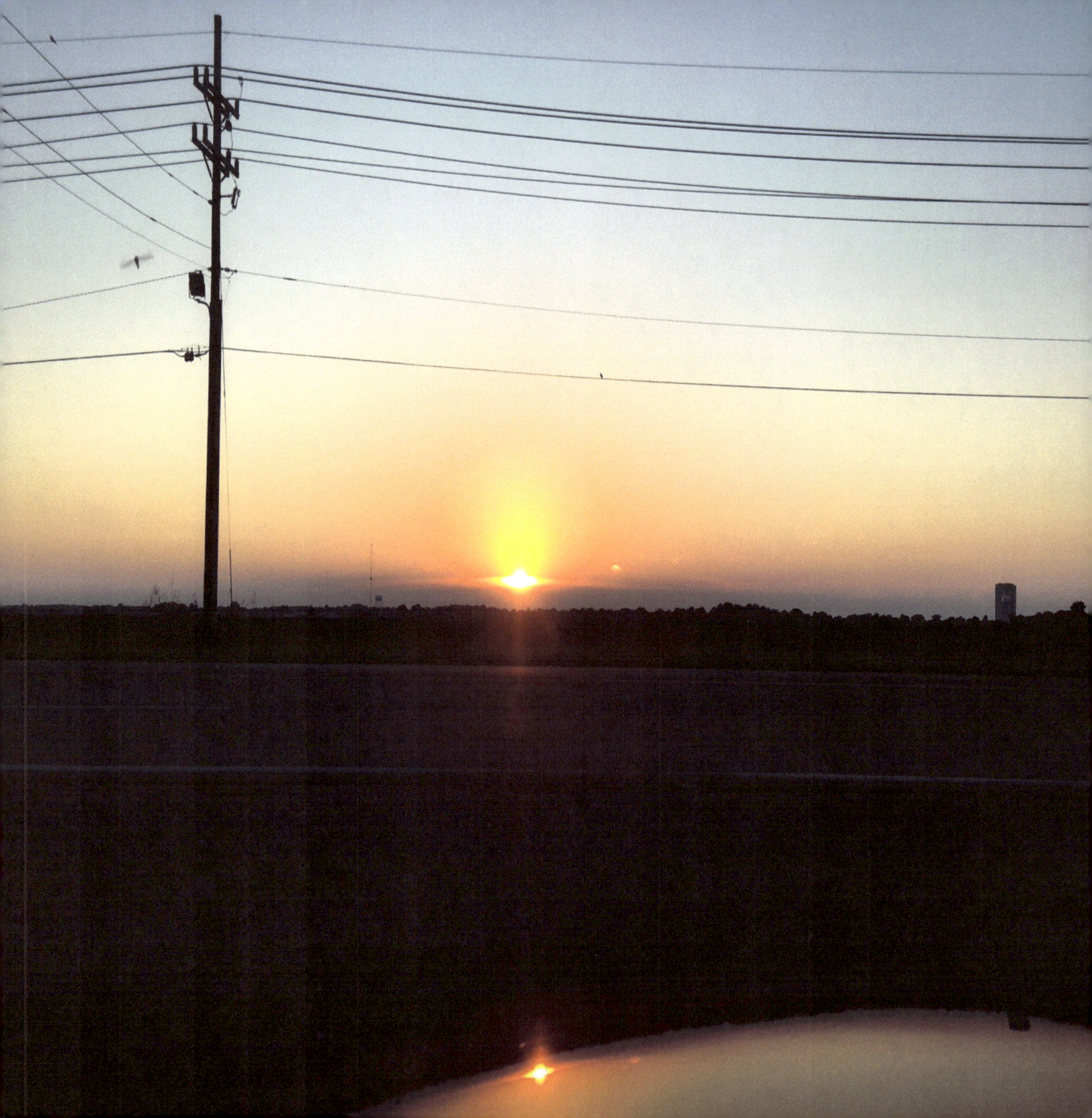

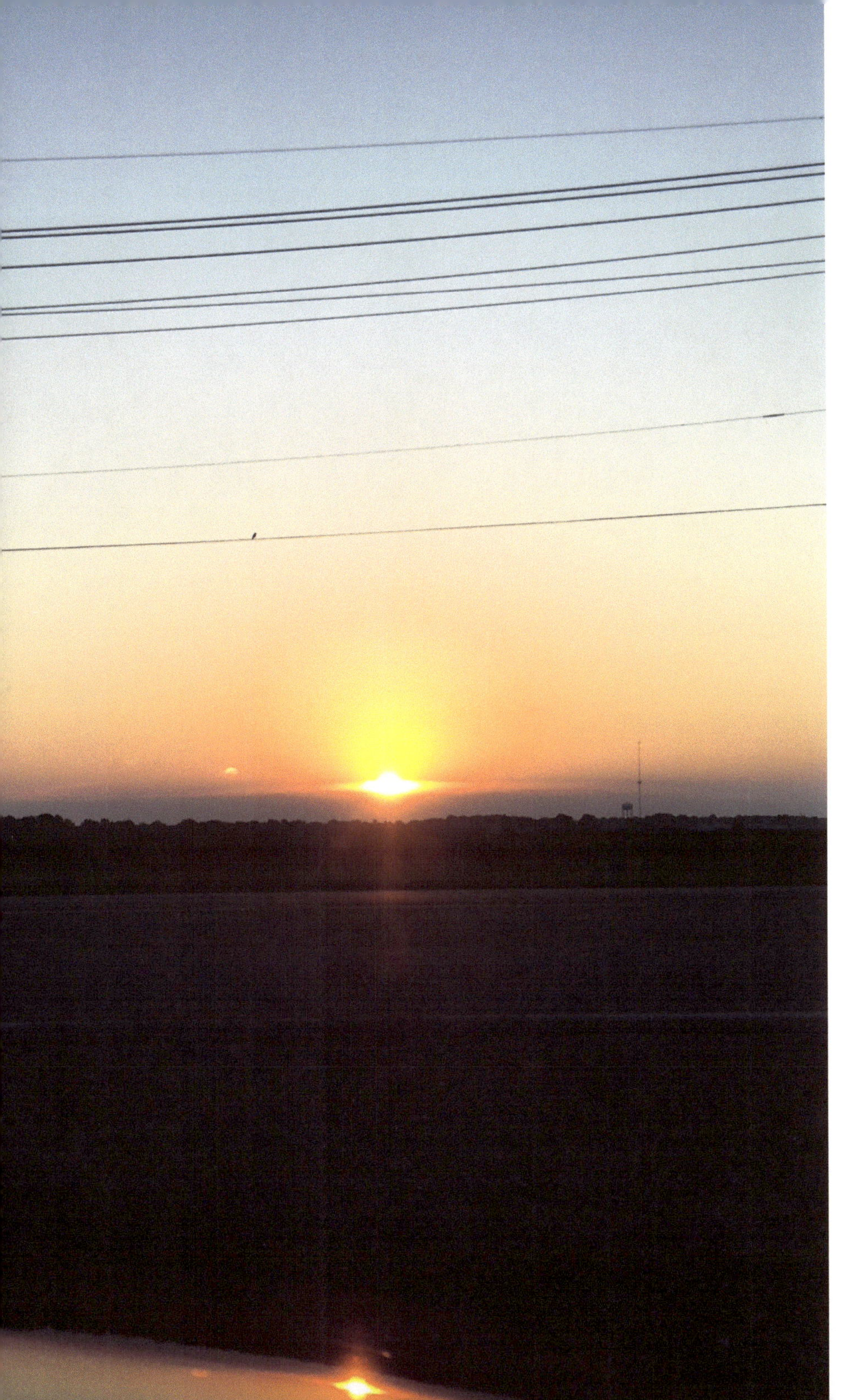

Sunny Side Up

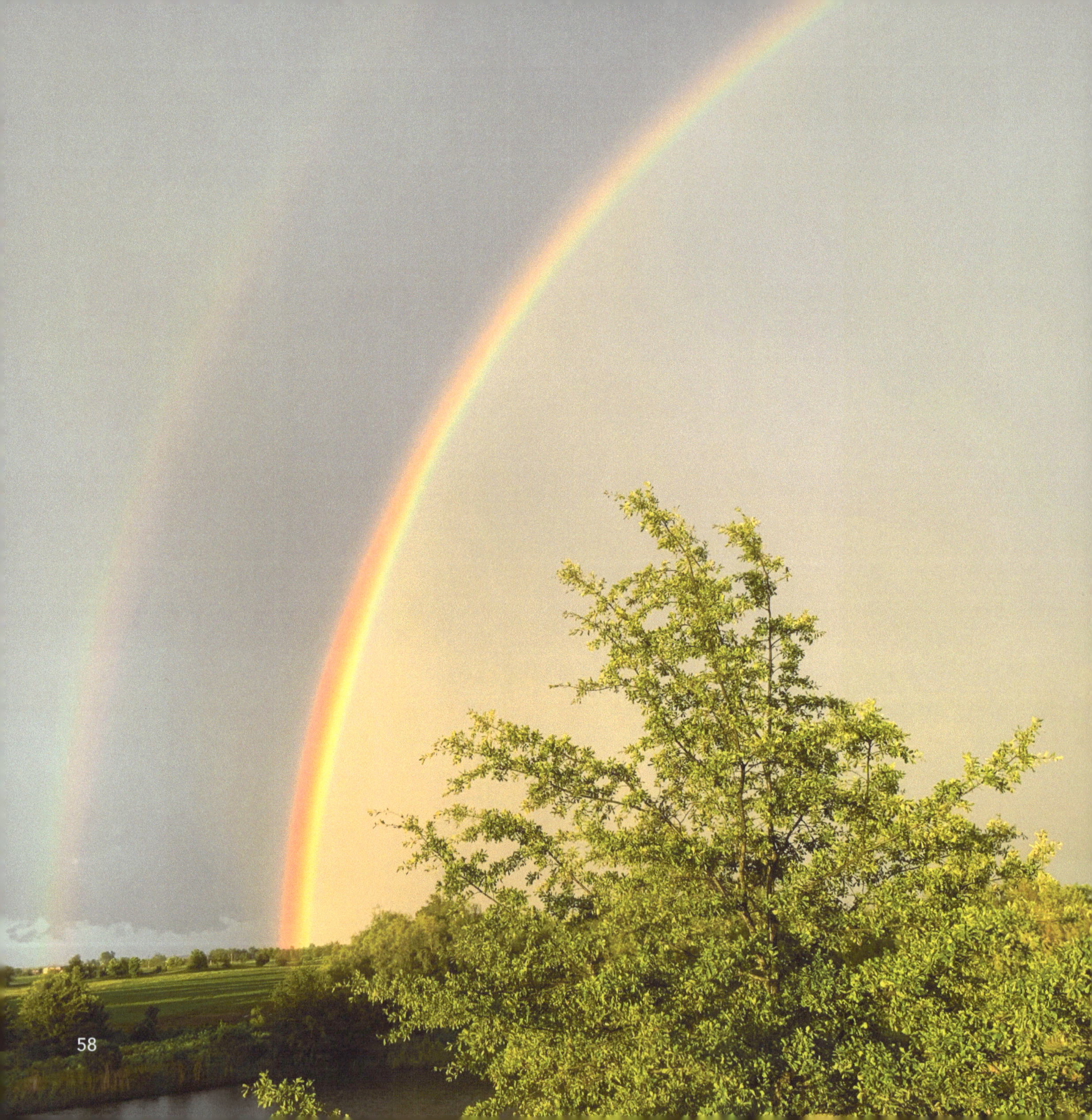

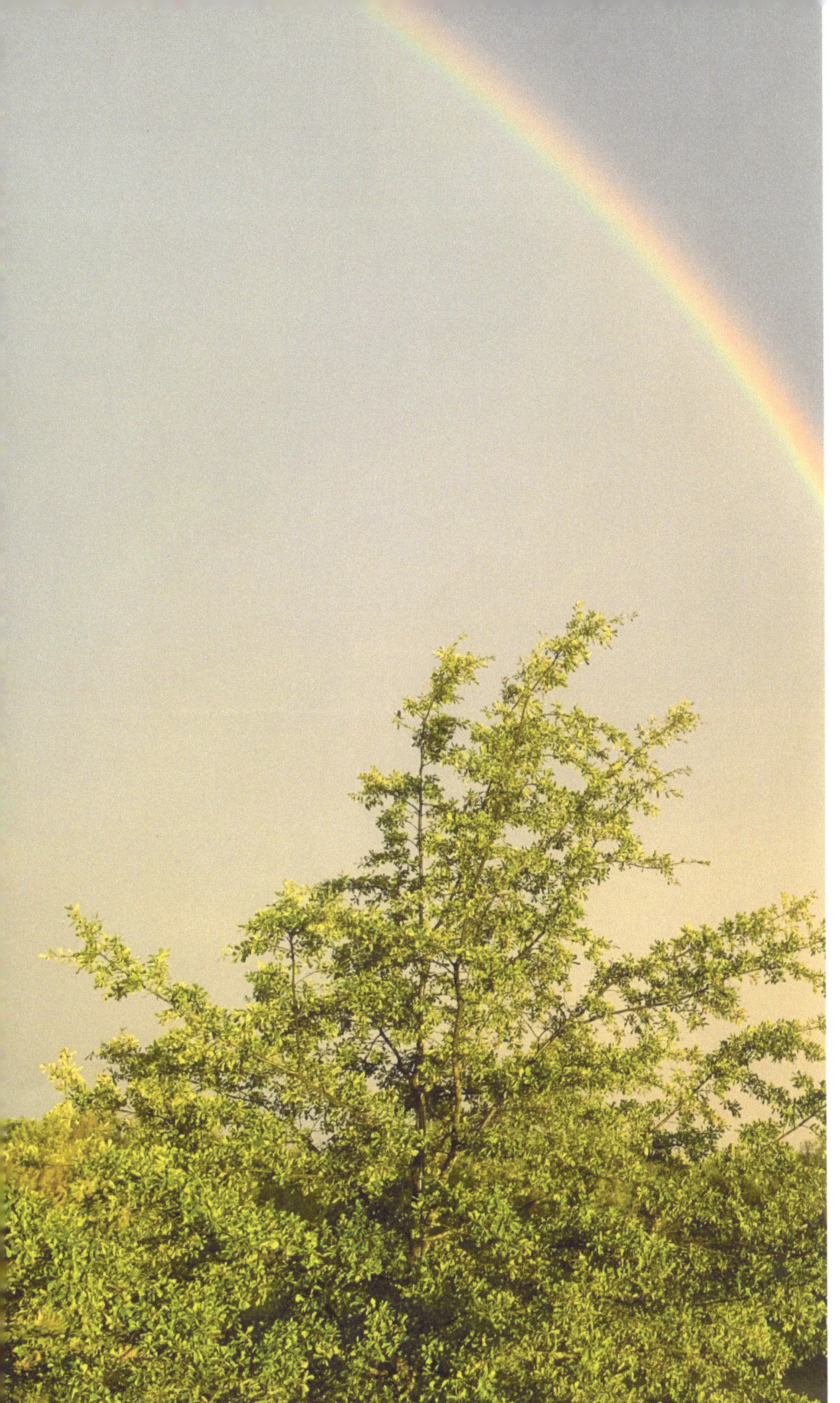

Double Pots of Gold

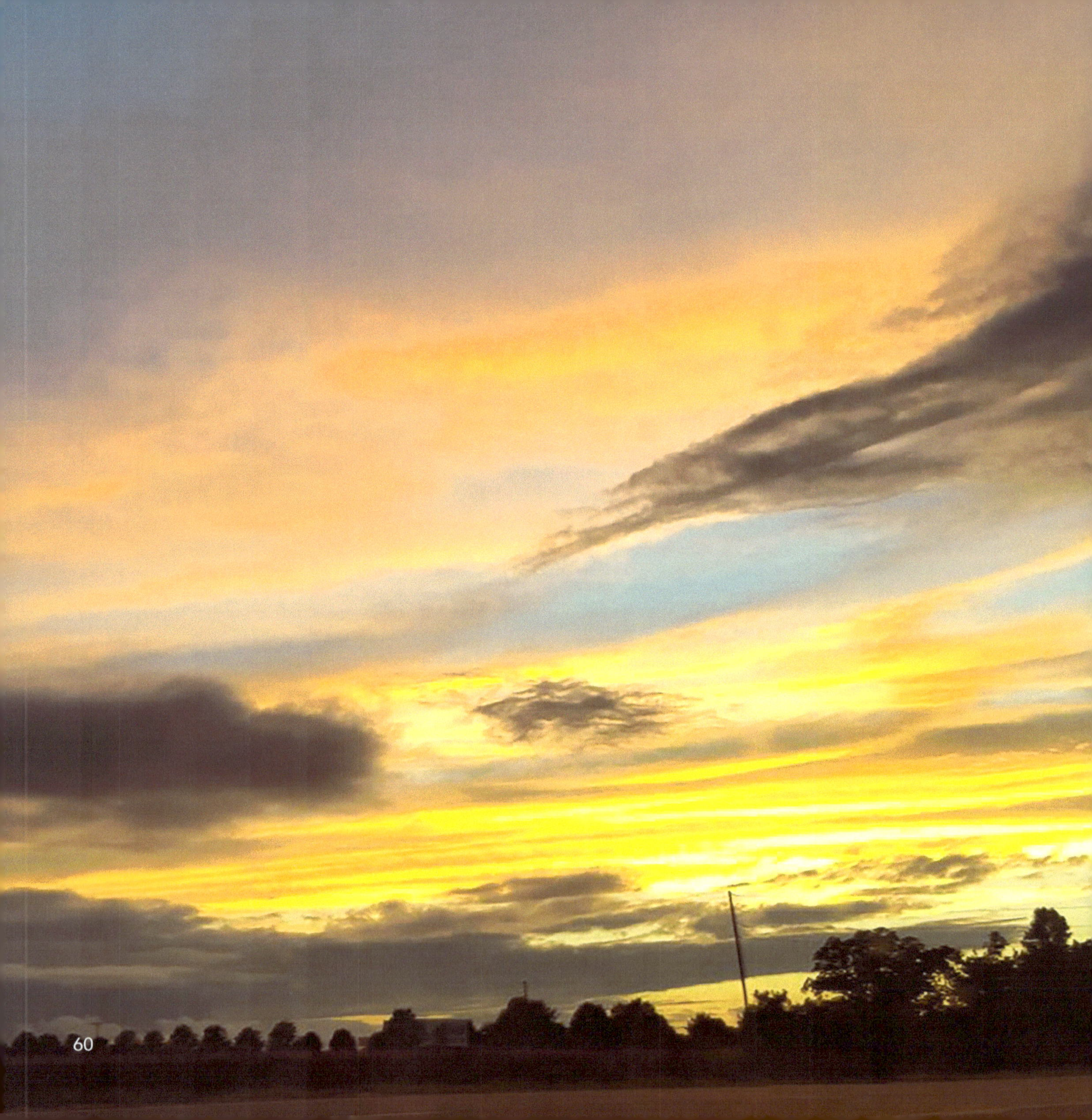

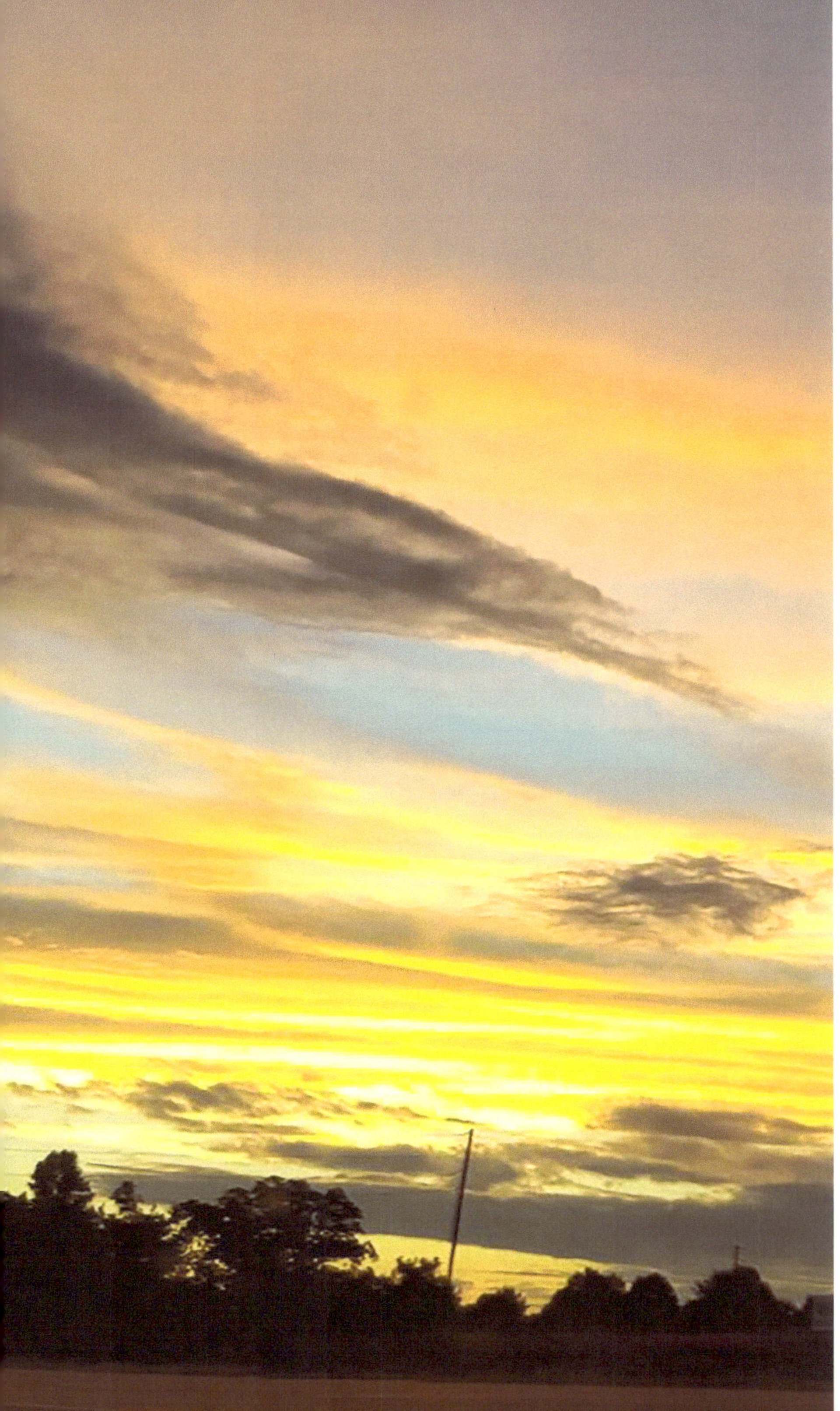

Look for Lemon-aid

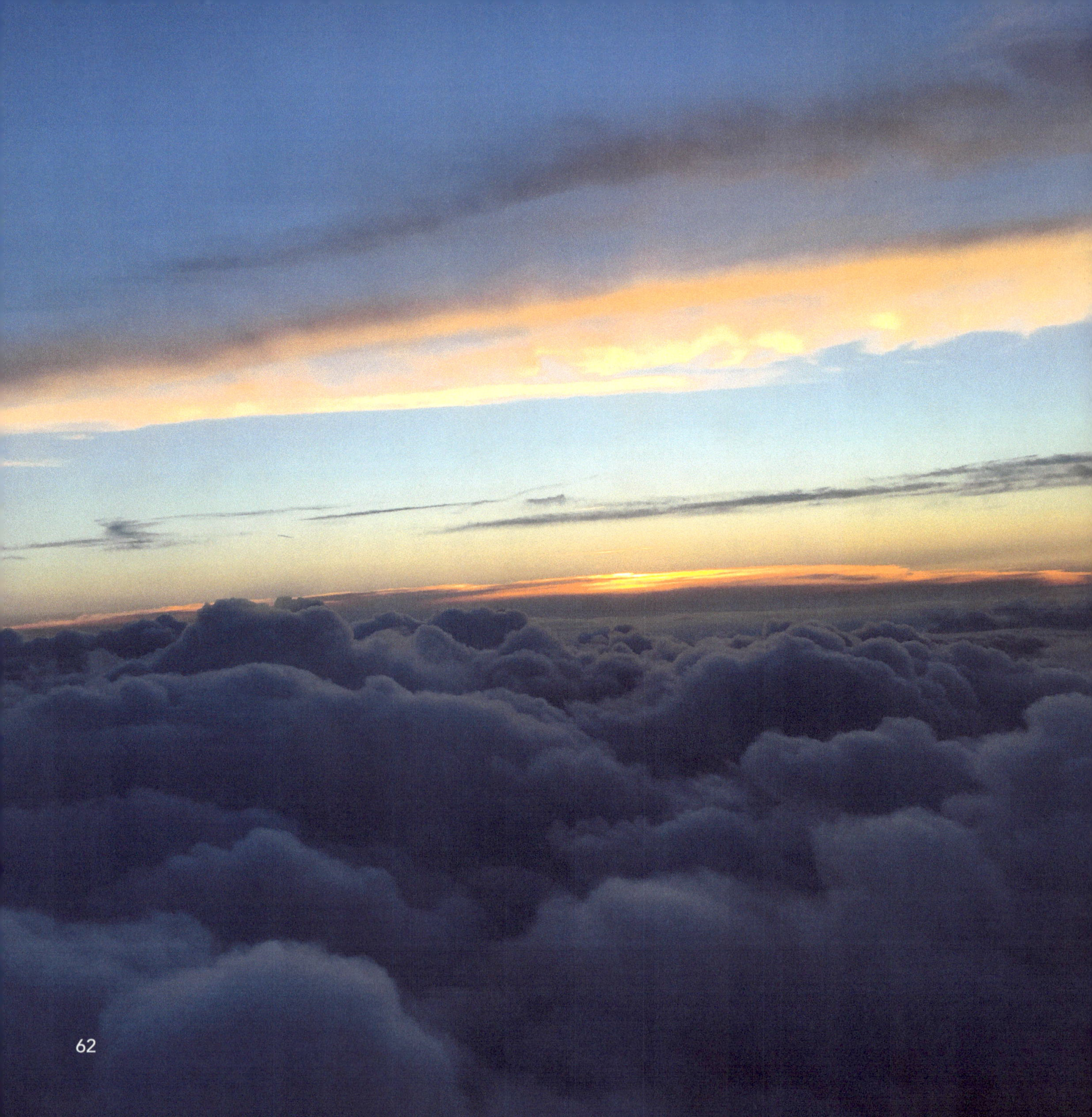

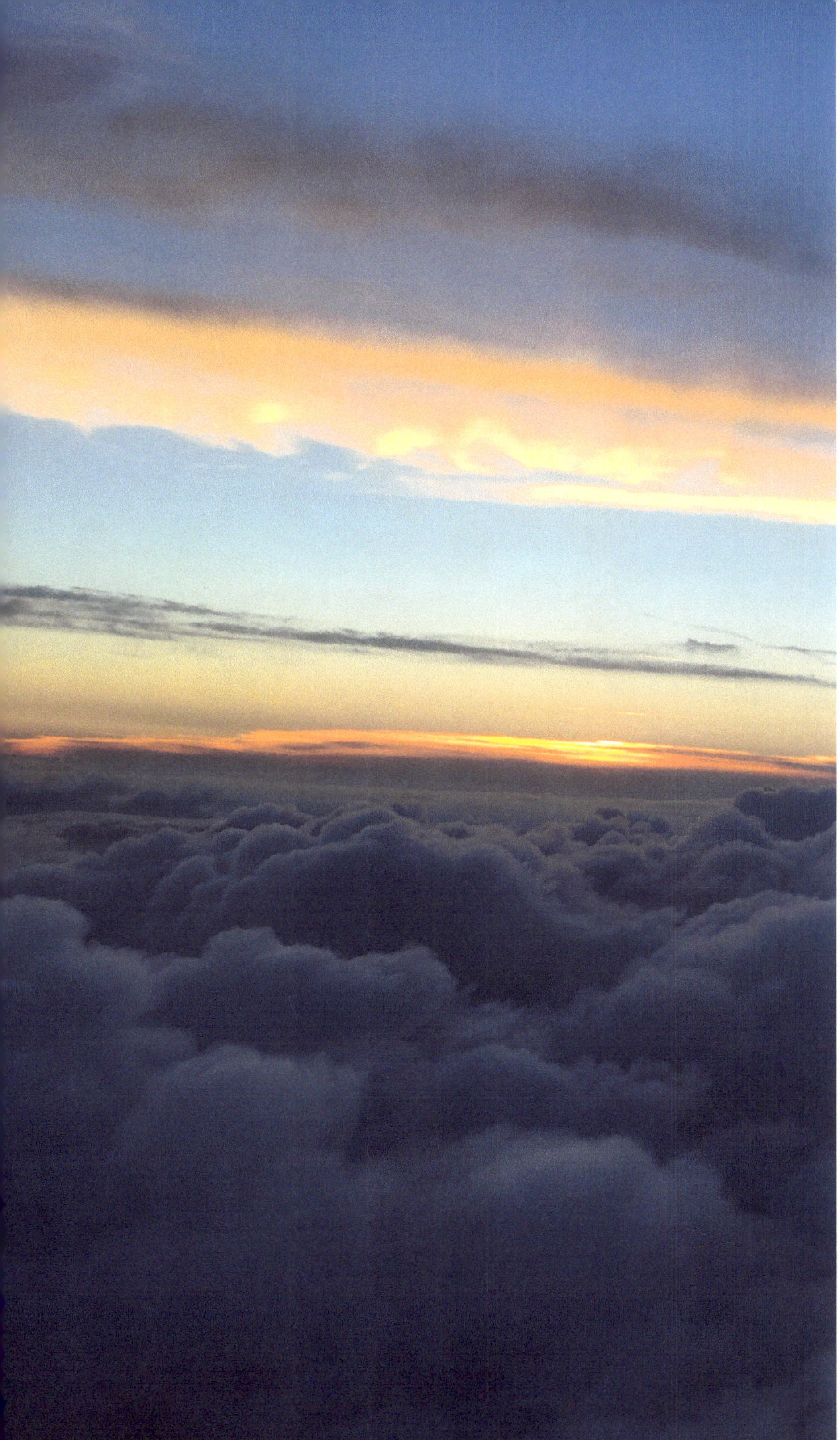

Cotton Candy Clouds

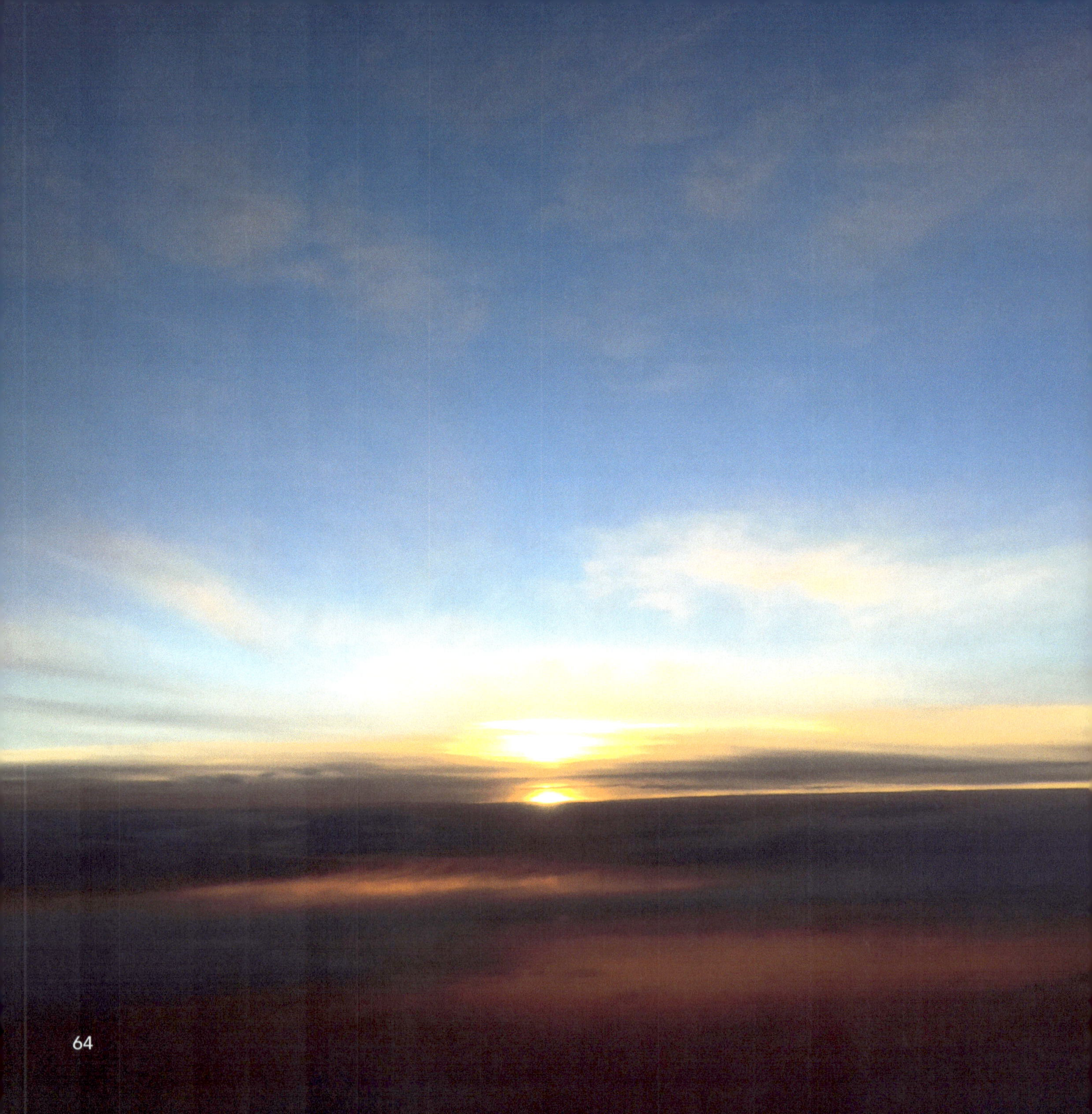

Shine Through

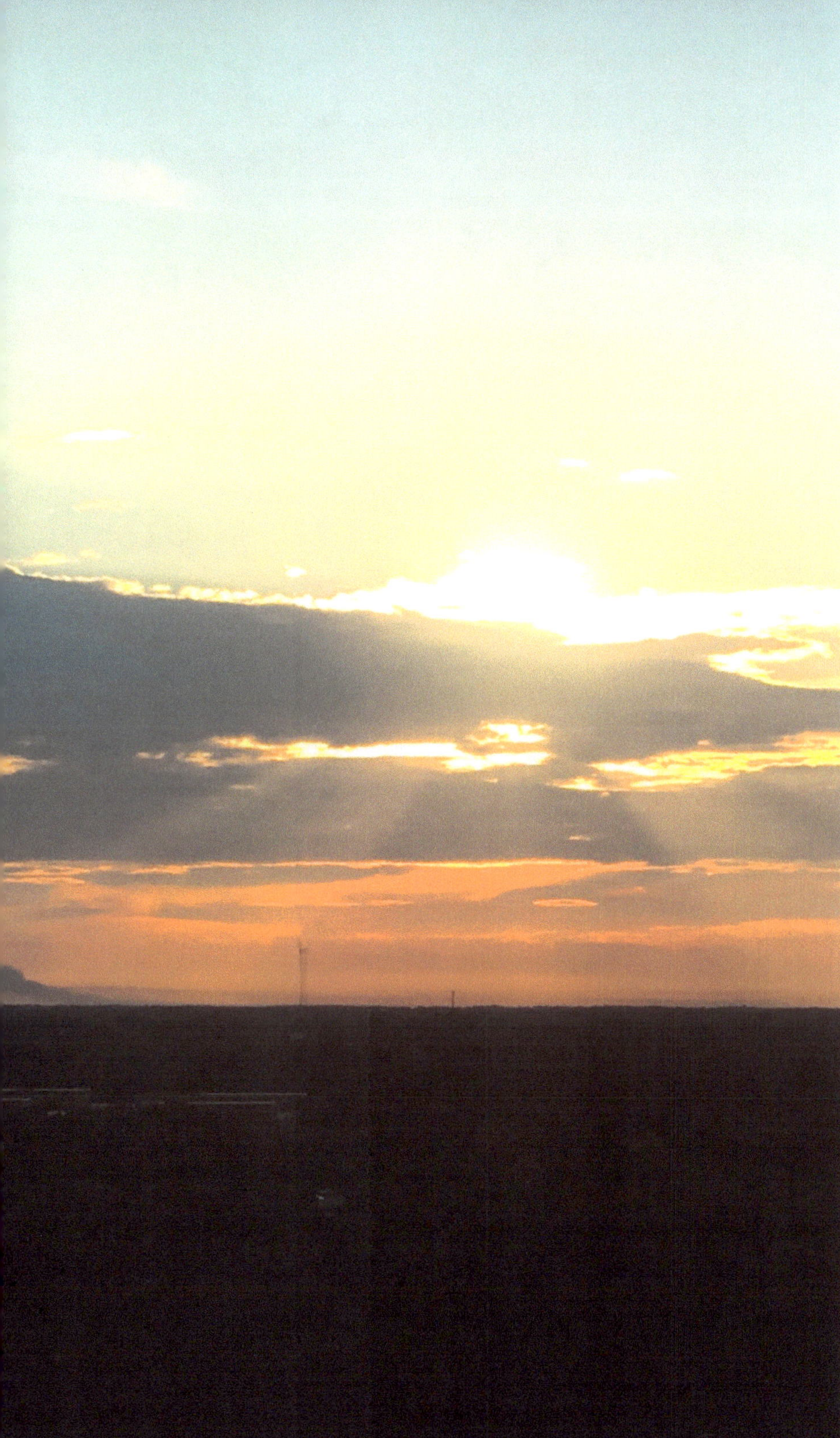

Radiate

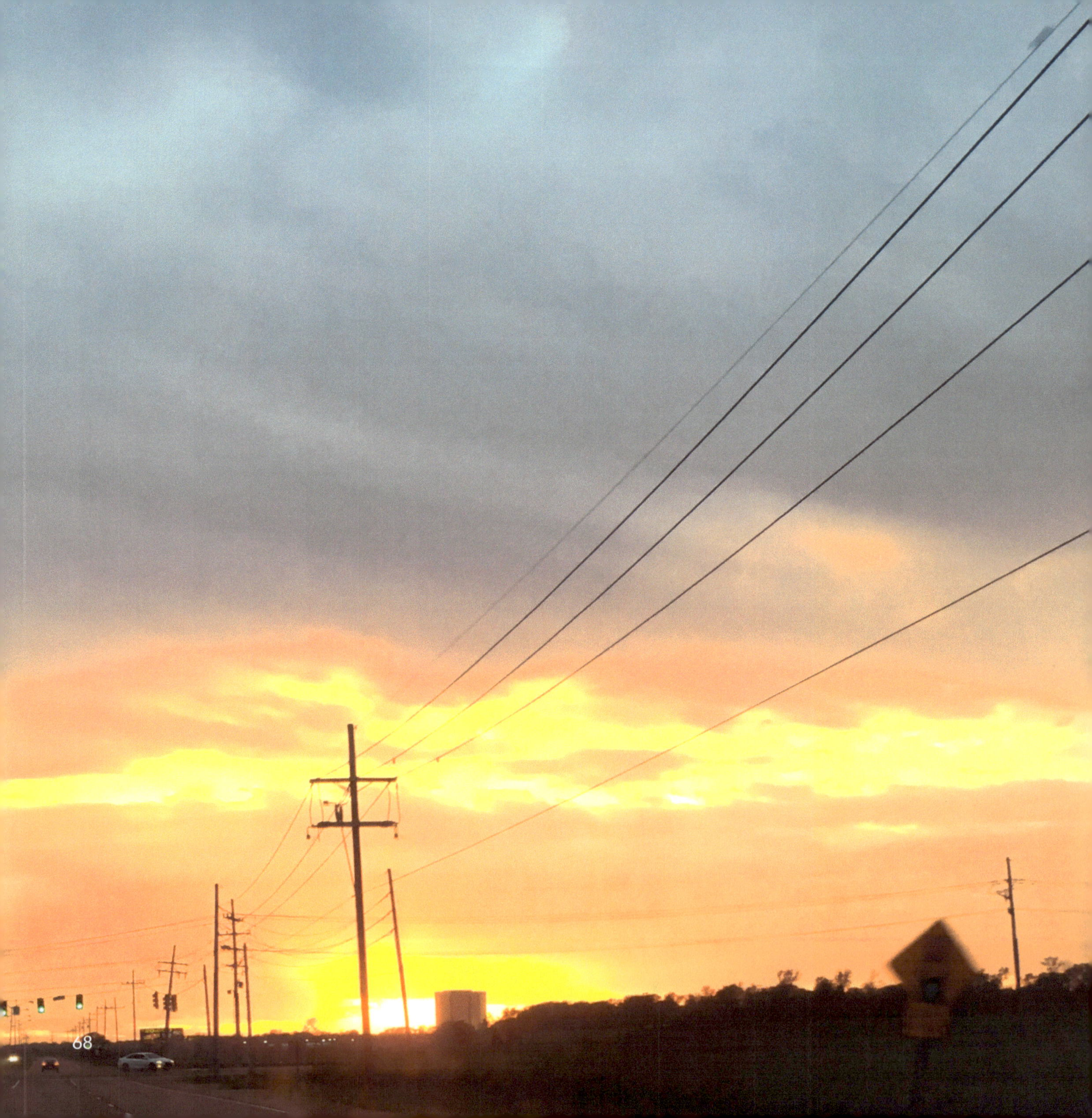

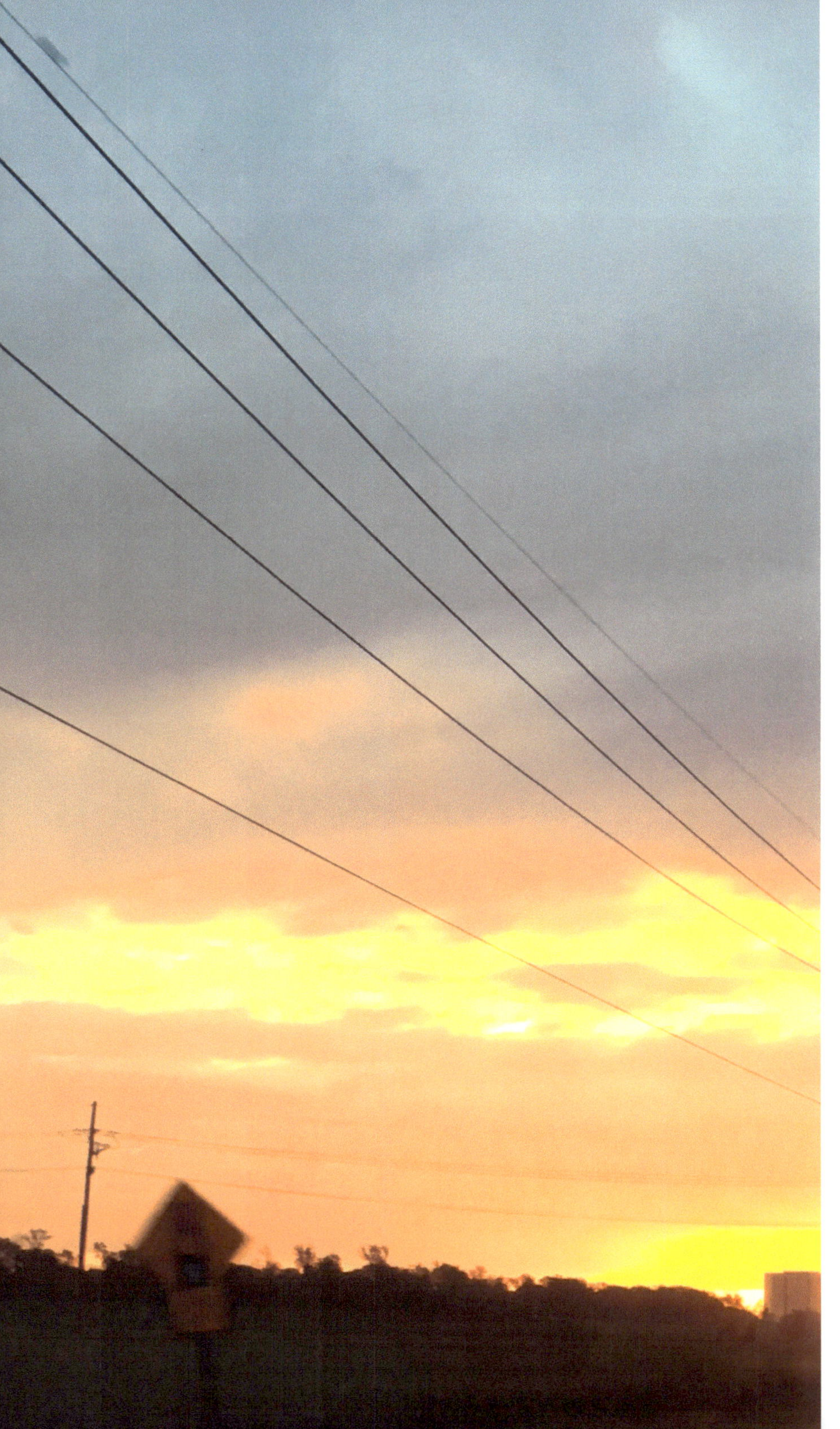

Southern Sherbet

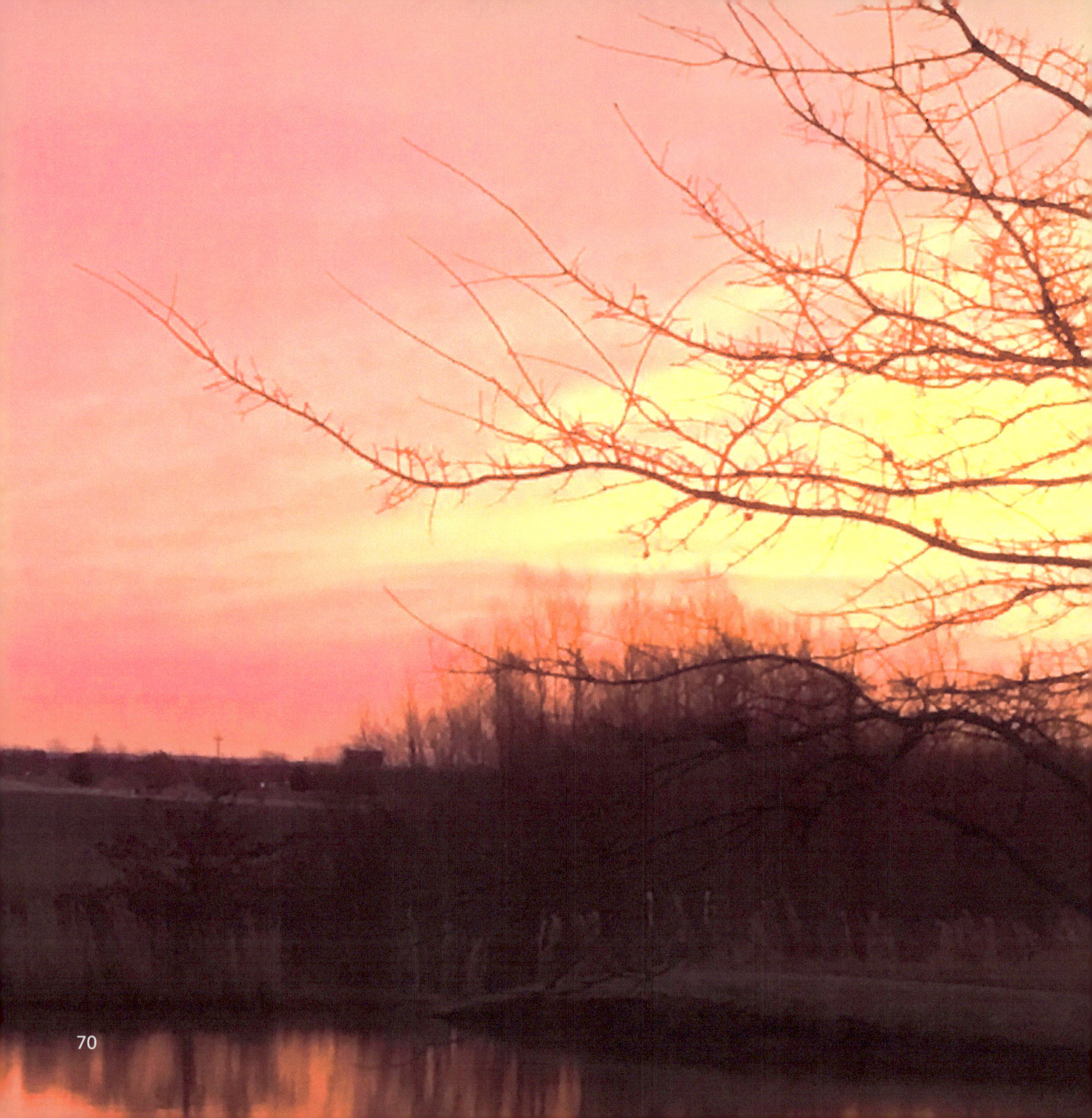

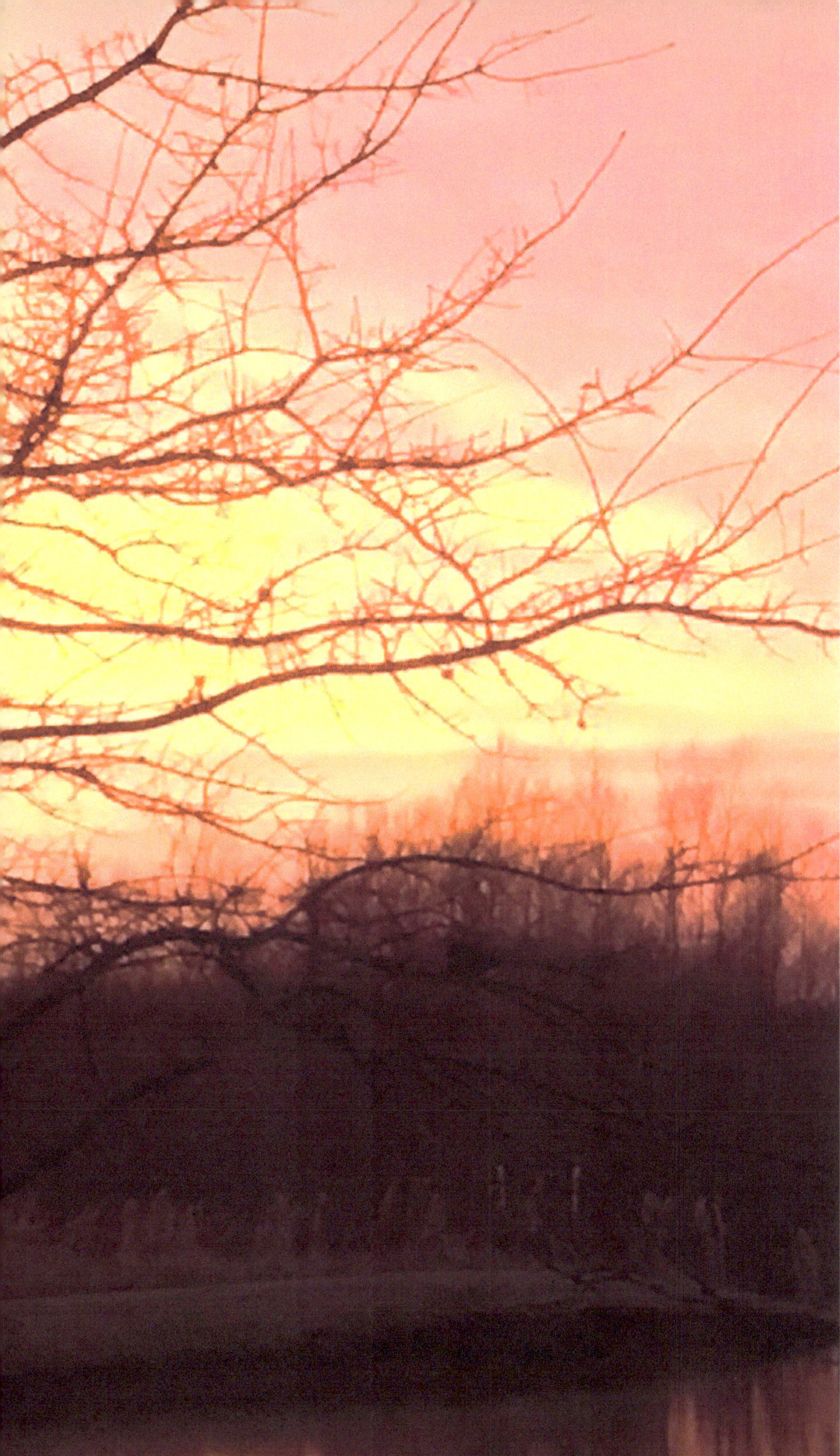

Watermelon Skies

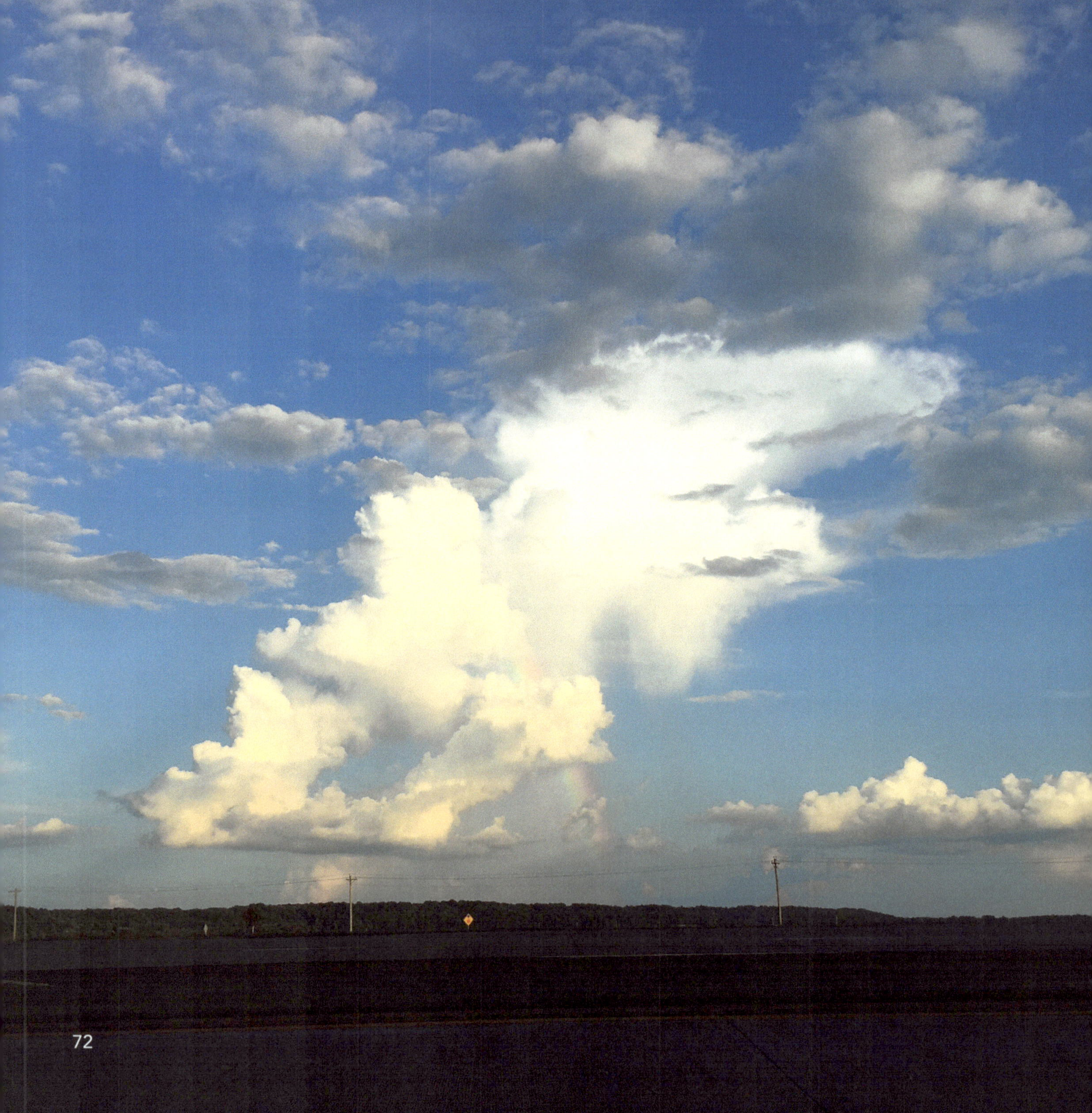

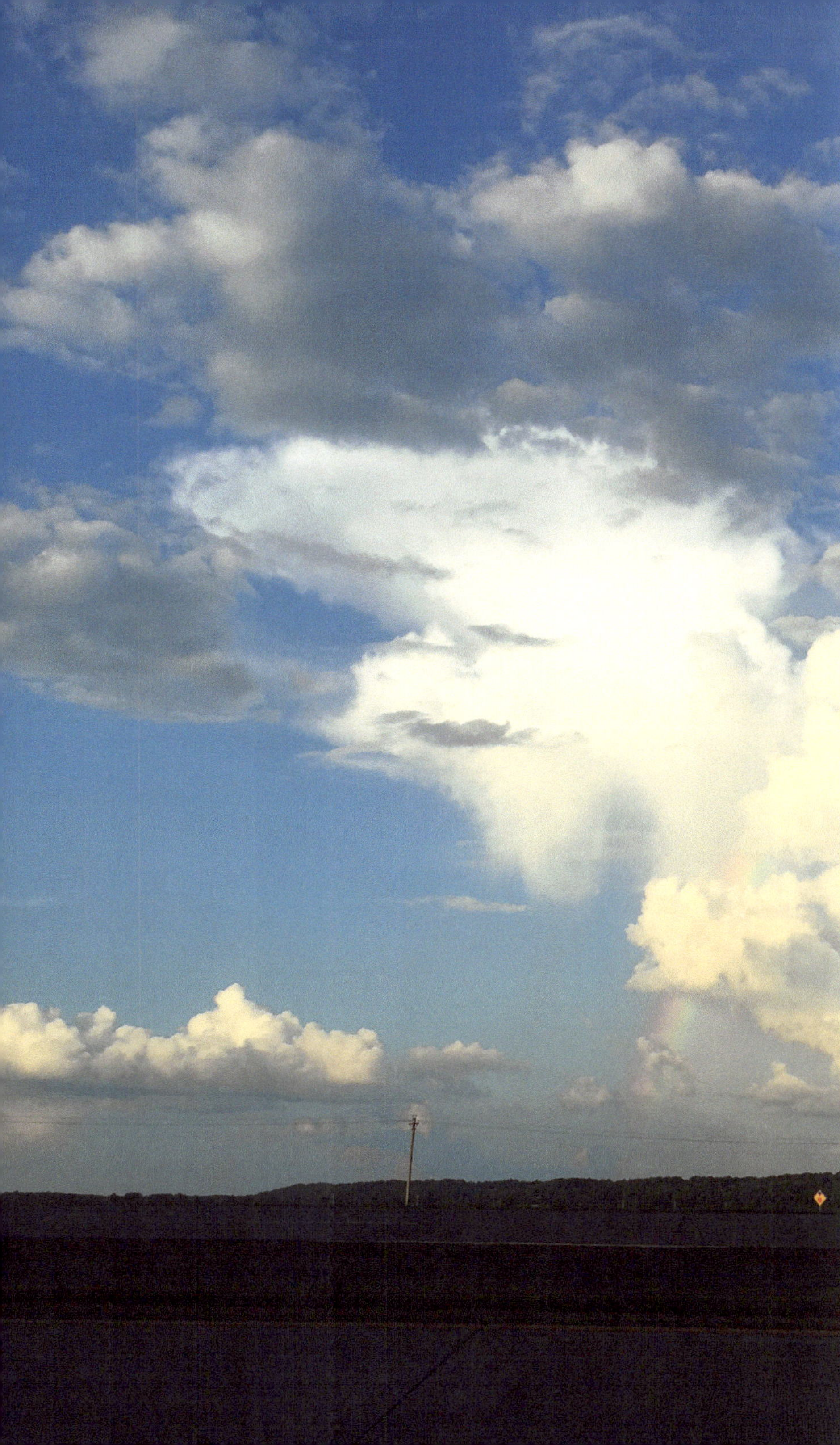

Find the Rainbow

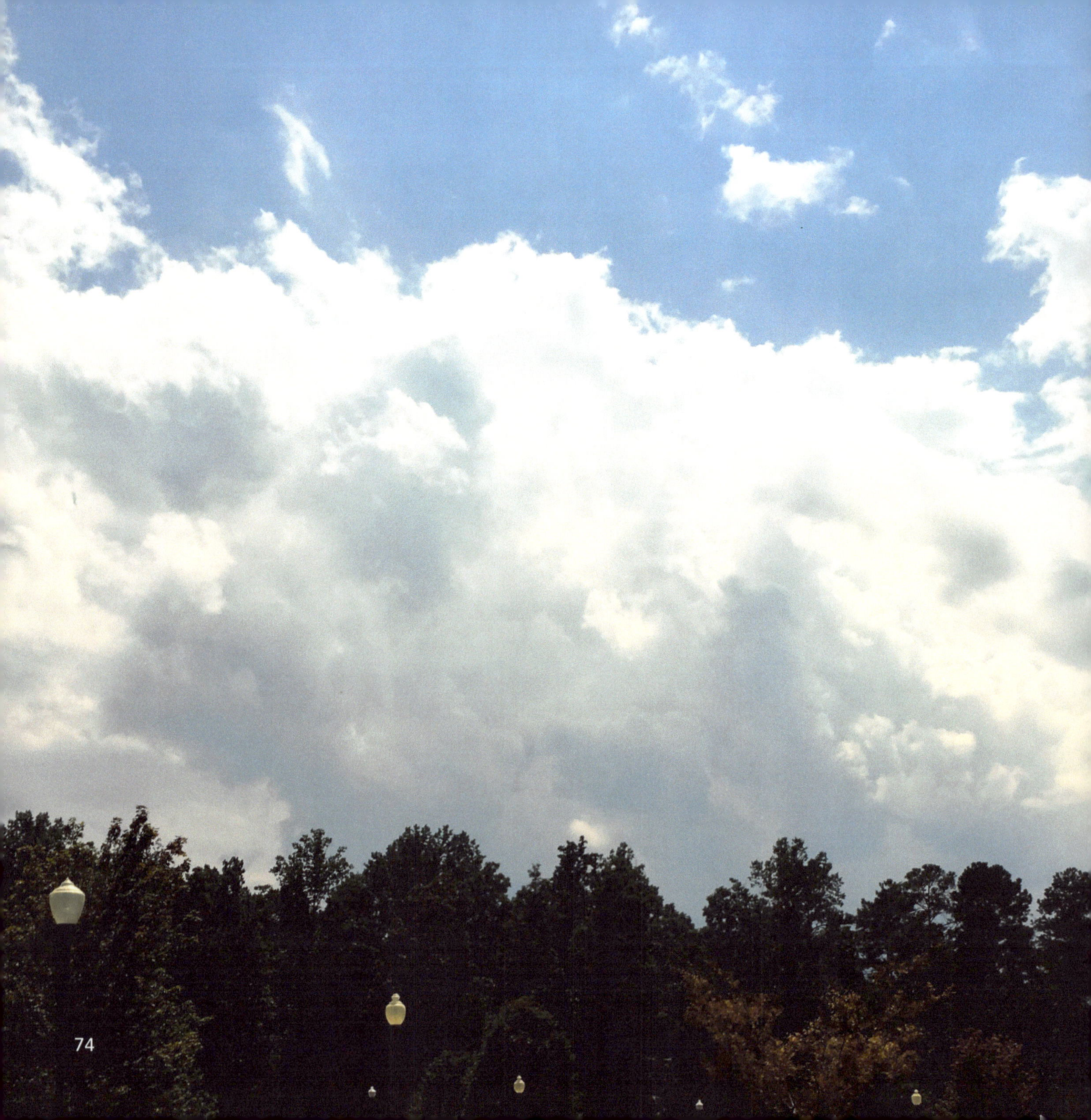

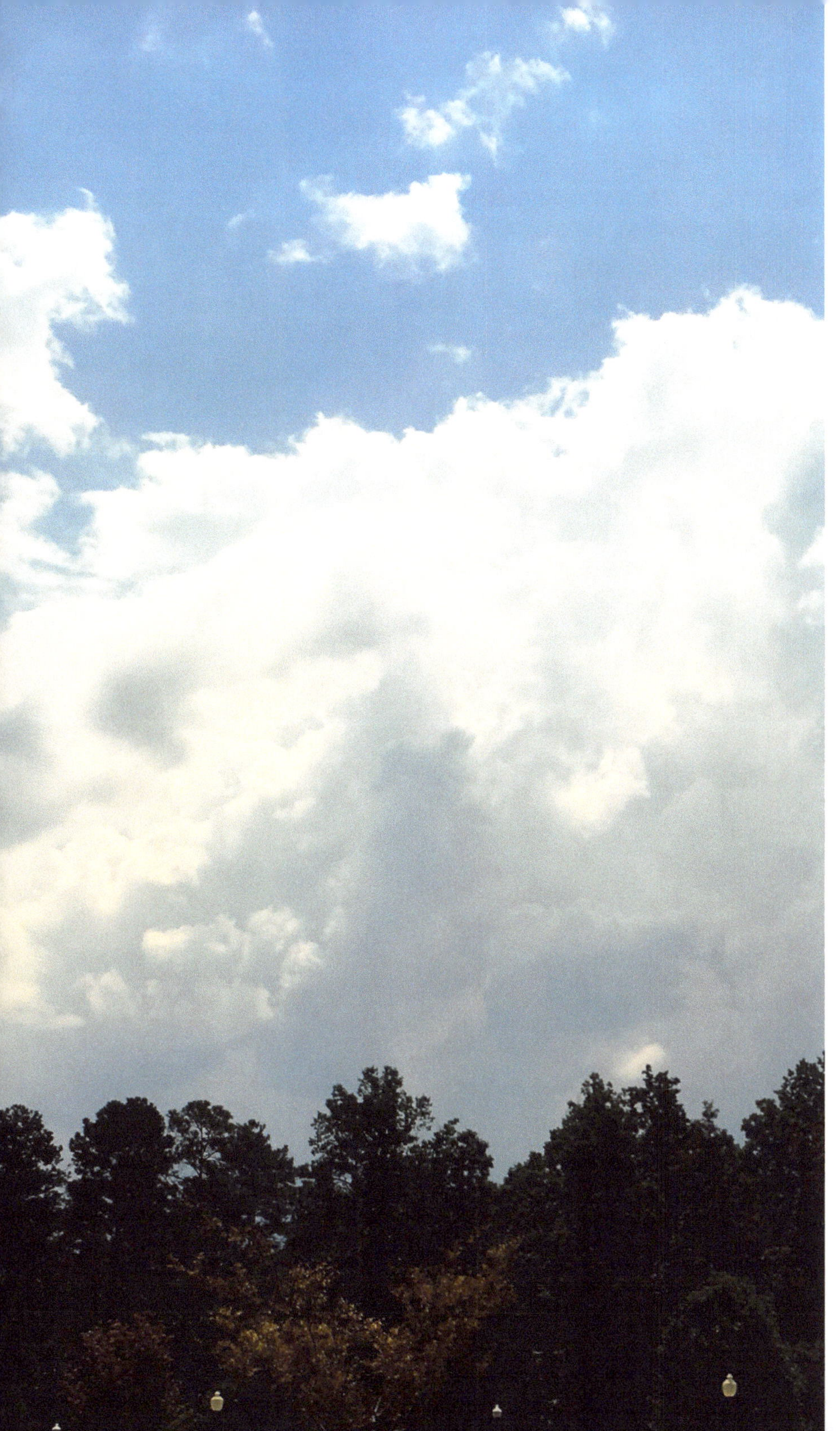

Stand Tall

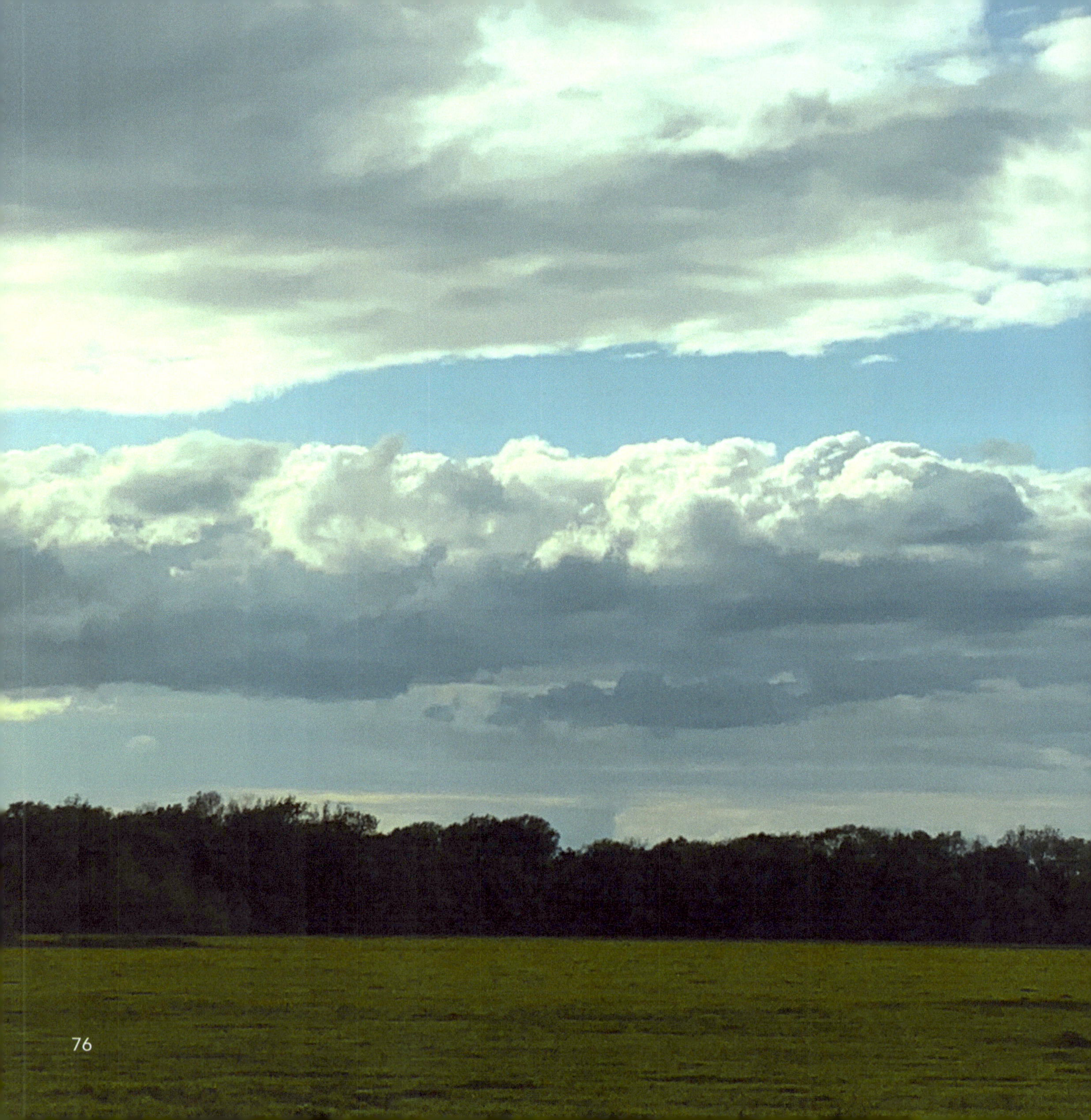

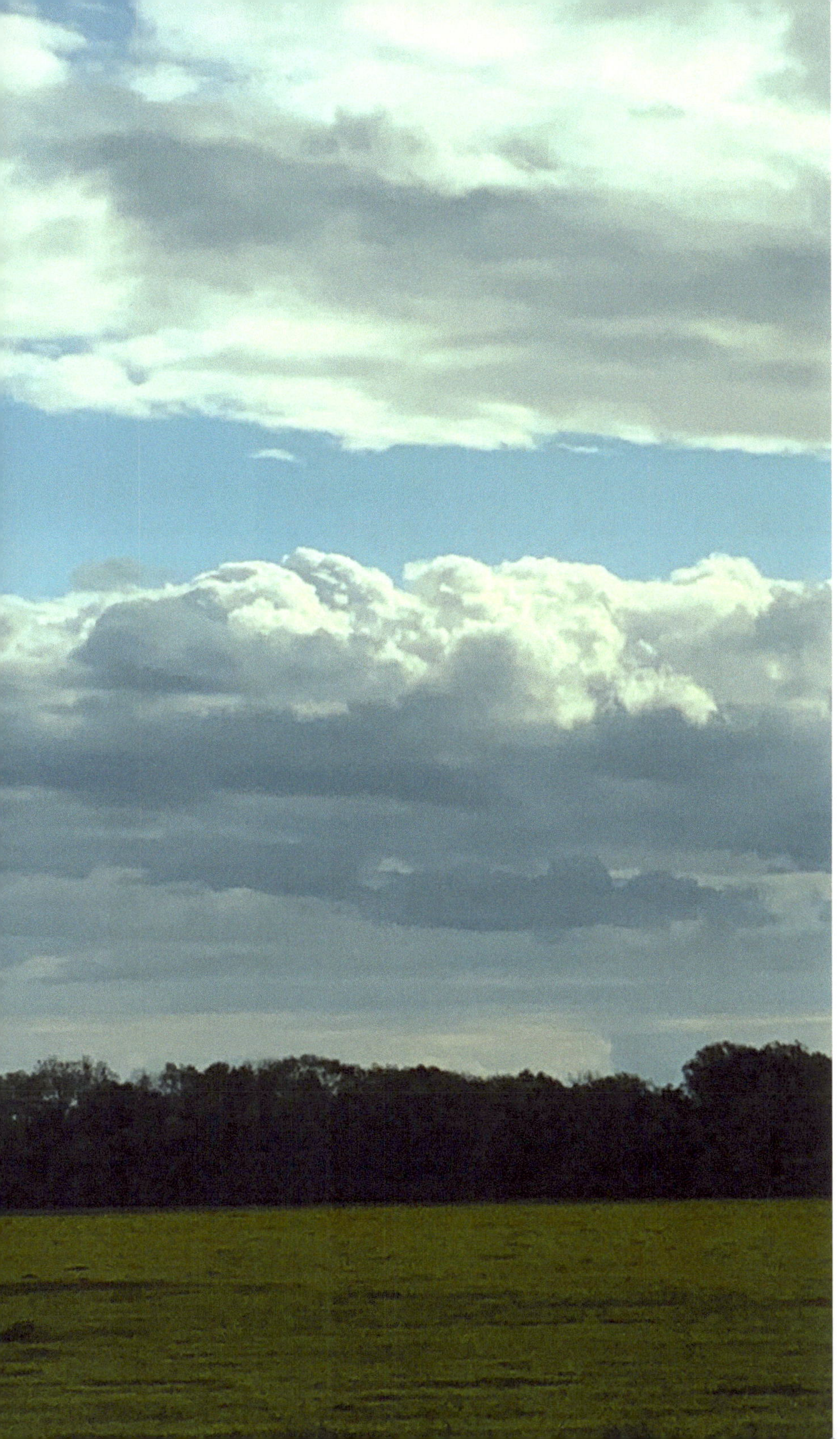

In Plane Site

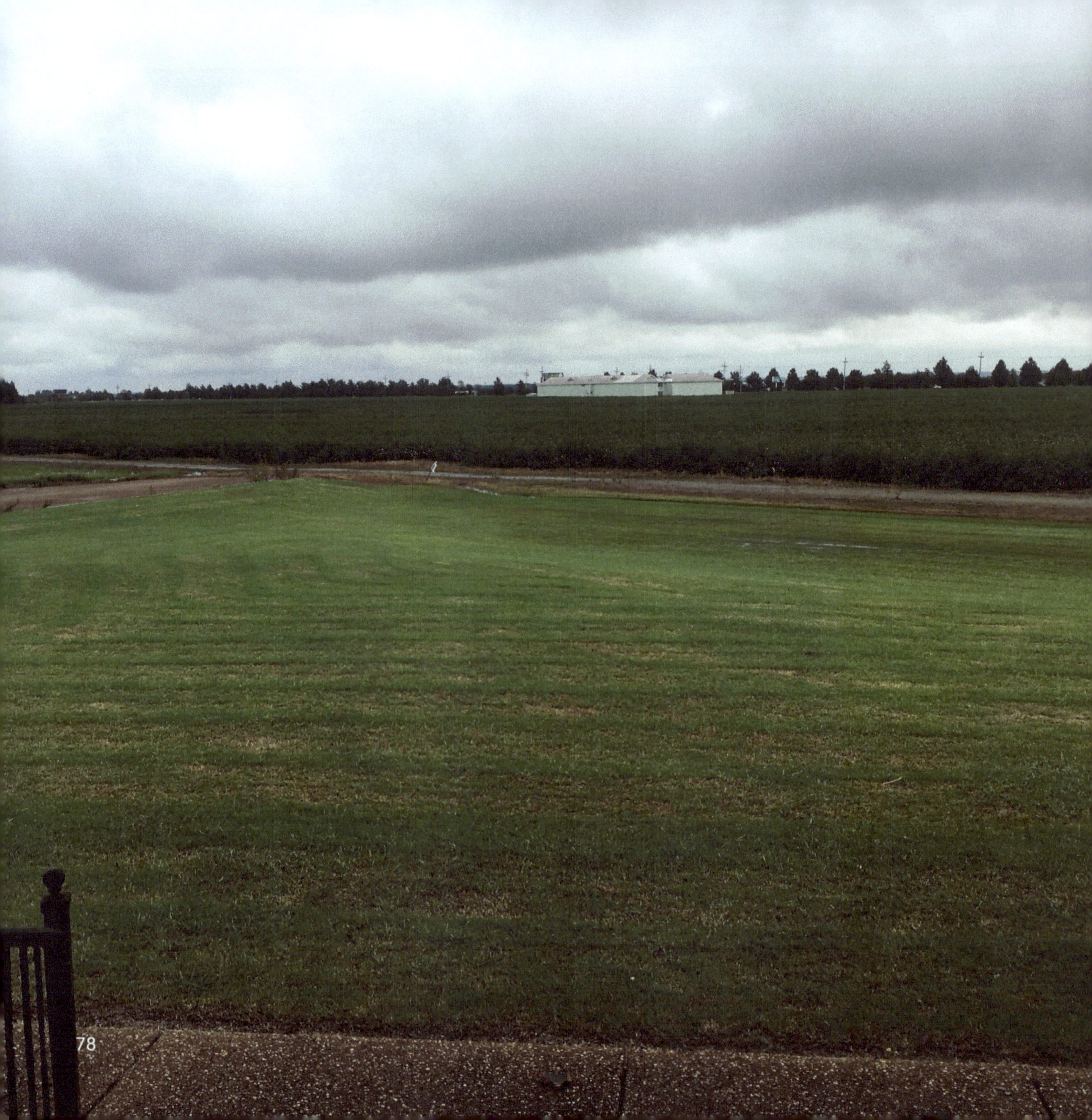

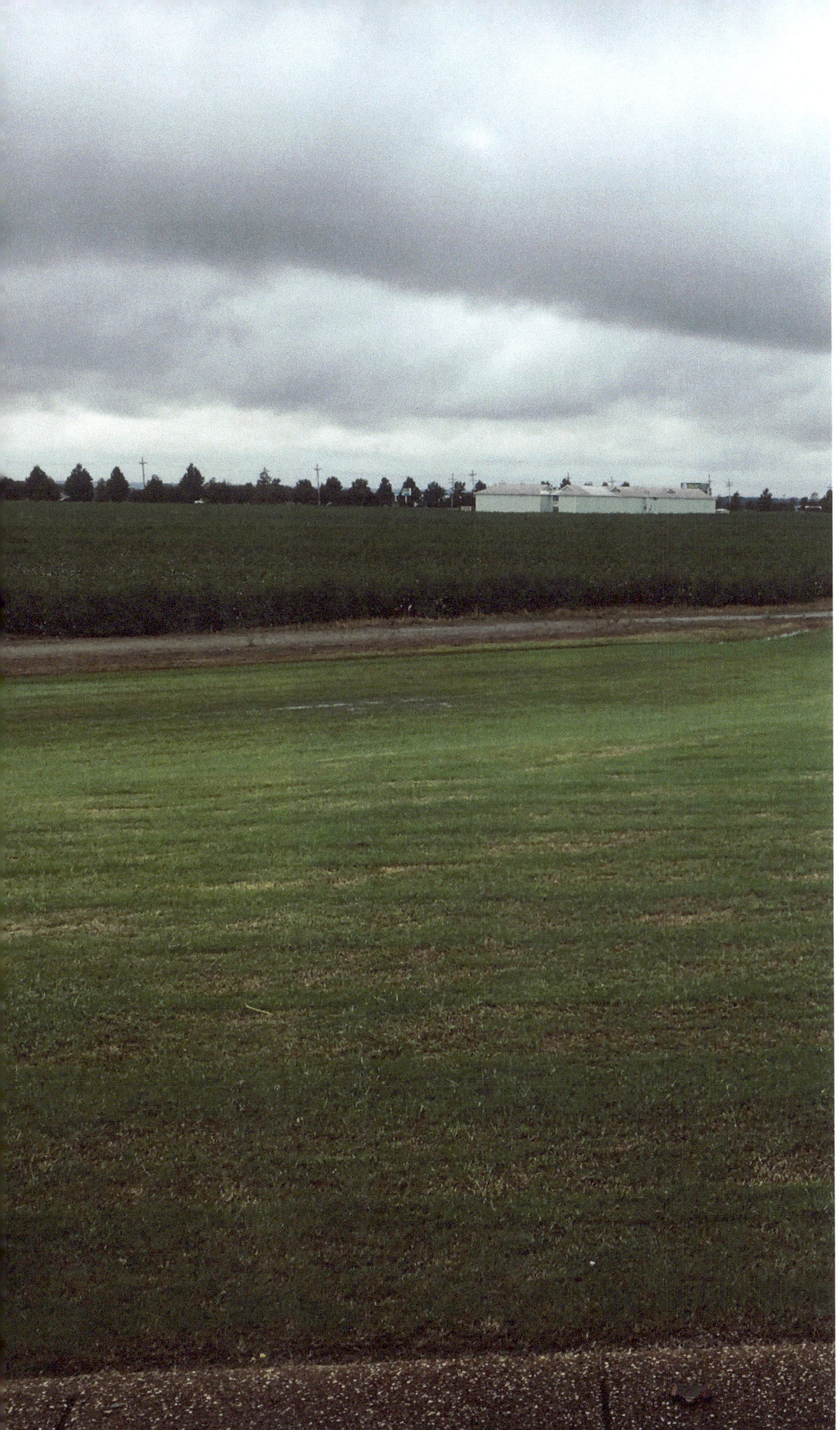

High Cotton Skies

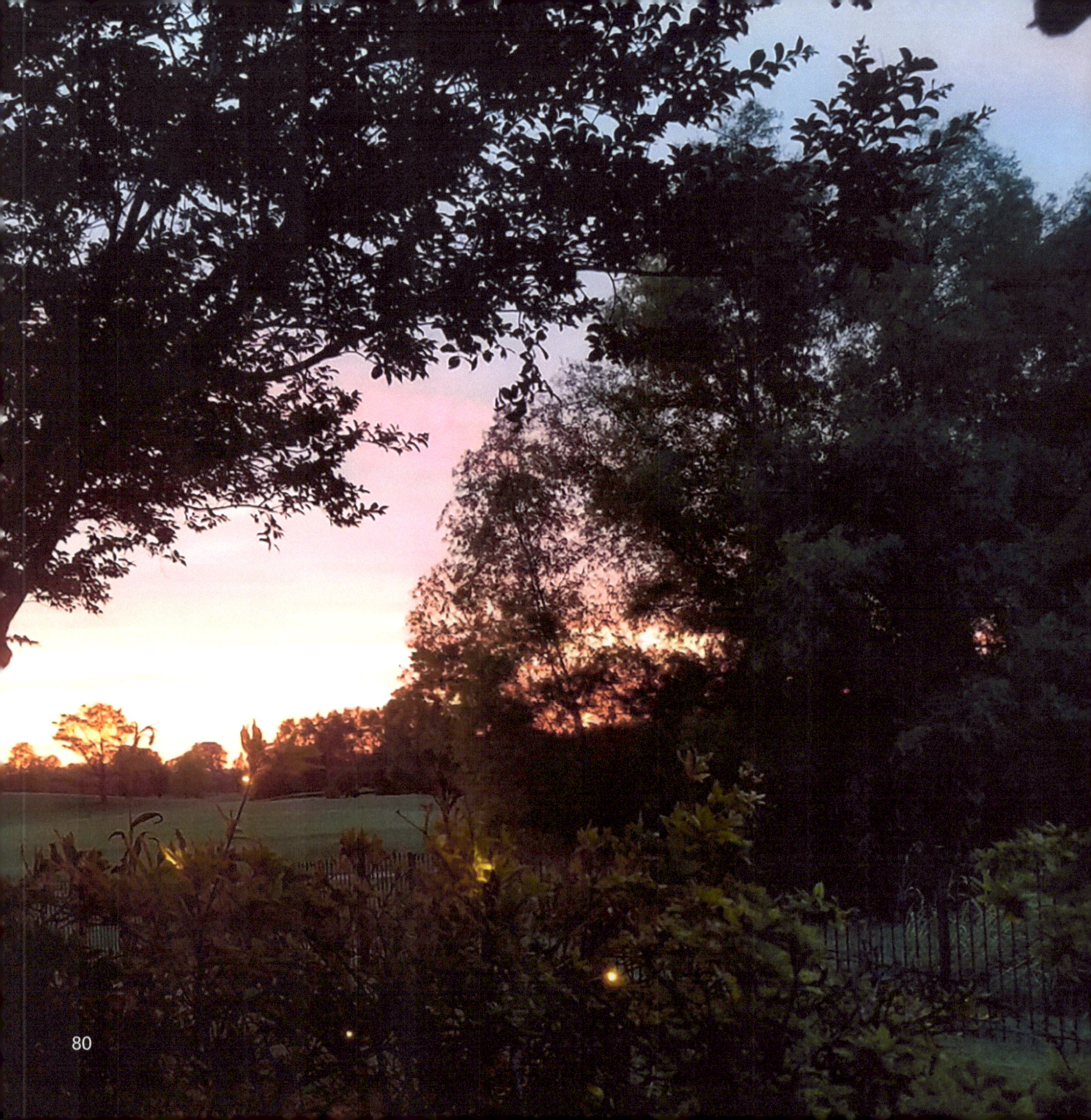

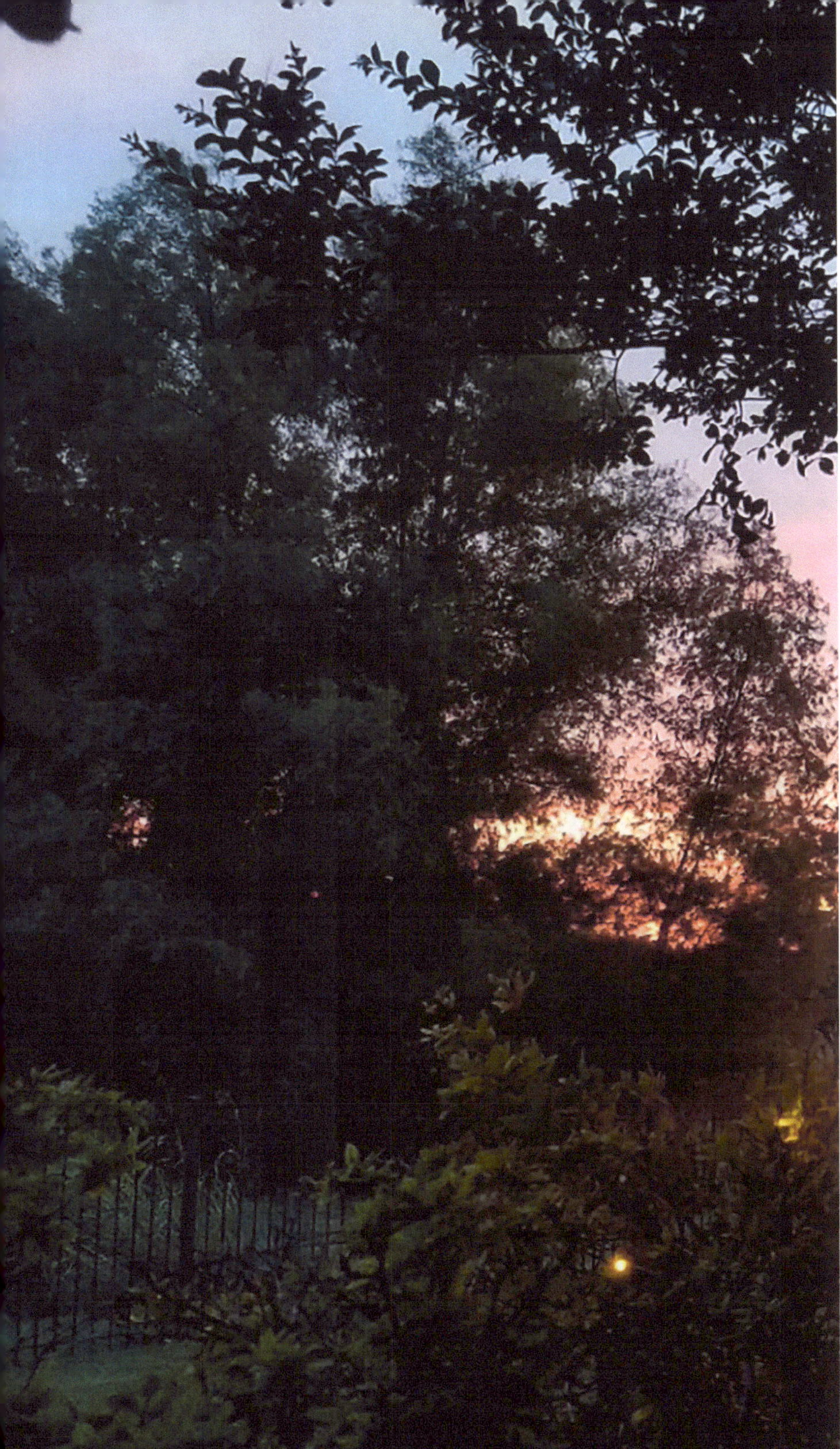

Vette's Veranda

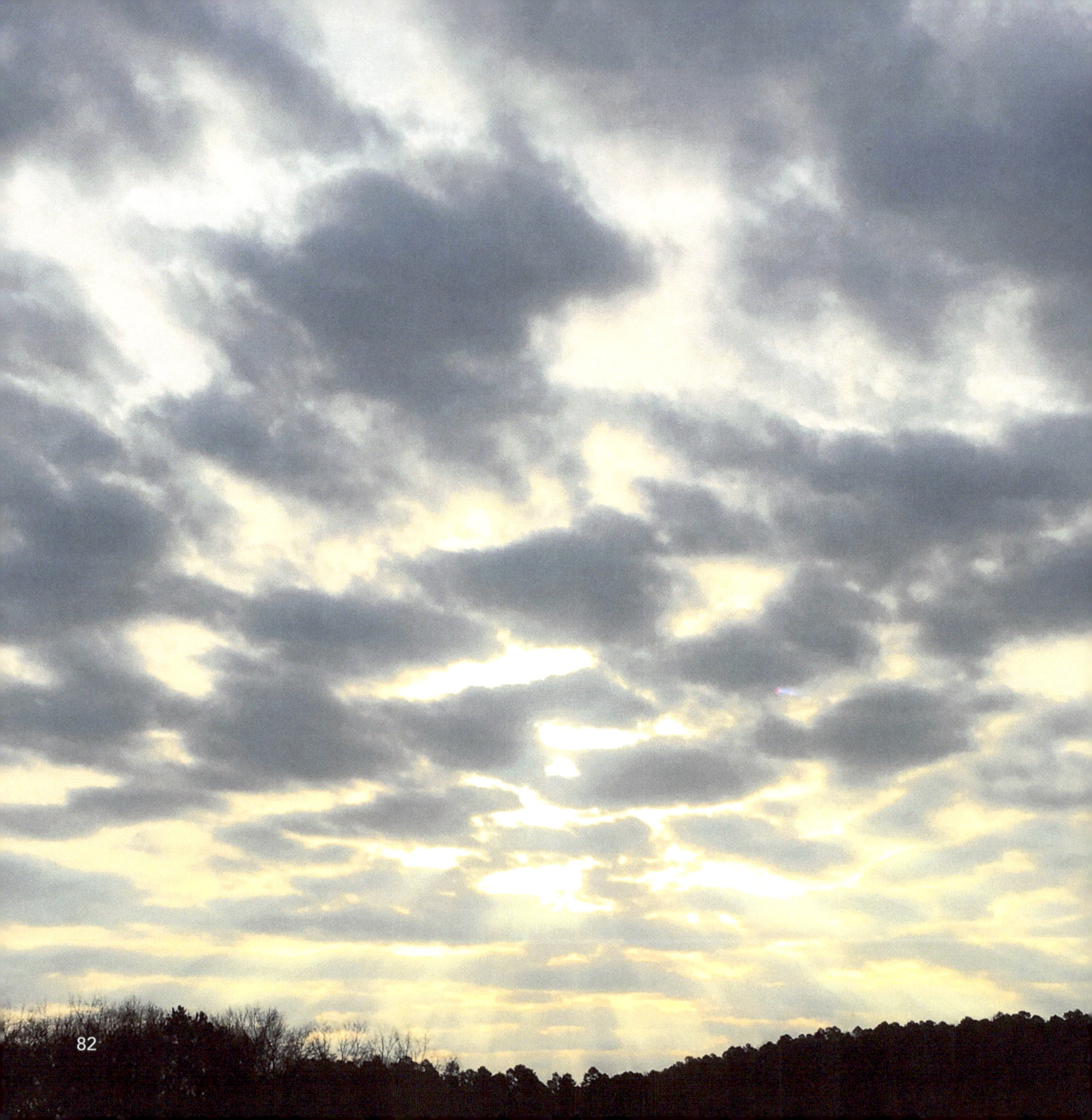

3
LOOK UP

As a writer and an author, it's relatively simple for me to write tons of words to describe my feelings, emotions and thoughts. An editor is, of course, my best friend.

With creating ***My Backyard Garden, Look up Mississippi***, a poem came to me from the universe. I look to the universe to always gives me what I need to share with you.

So this chapter is devoted to that poem: "Look Up - Way In the Middle of the Air."

The Poem:

"Look Up, Way In The Middle of the Air"

Look up Mississippi
Look up to the skies.
Cloud formations were there
When our ancestors died.
What will we leave
For our children to come,
A history of death or a history of love.

Yes, despite our difference
All our forefathers and foremothers died,
With prejudice, hatred, fear, or pride.
One way or another, we all live and die.
What skies will our future look up to,
Reprise?

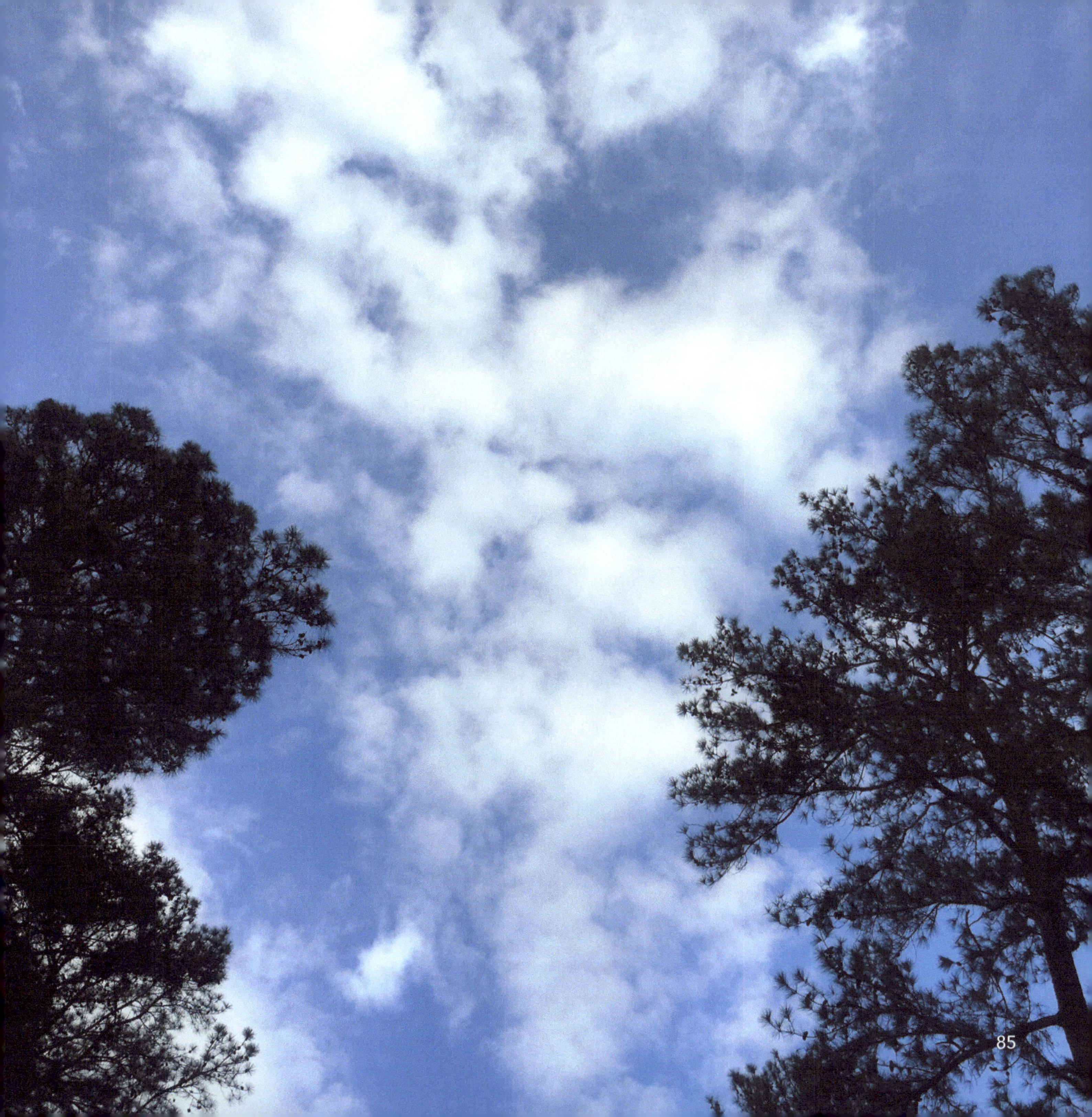

Here in the deep south
With a reputation worldwide,
We've learned that our ghosts
Of the past are alive.

Is there room for division
When it's all said and done?
Will we continue a legacy
Or reset like the sun
That blesses this land
With regrowth at each dawn?

Look up, Mississippi.
Look up to the skies,
For a promising wheel,
It's a flag, in our midst.
Let it heal the divide.
And sunset the myth.

by Debra Hester

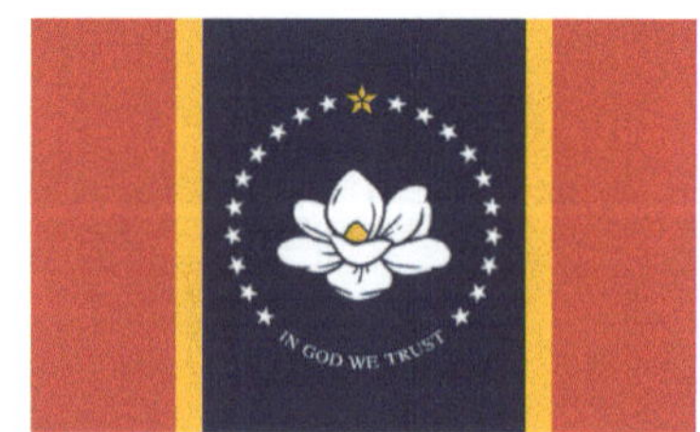

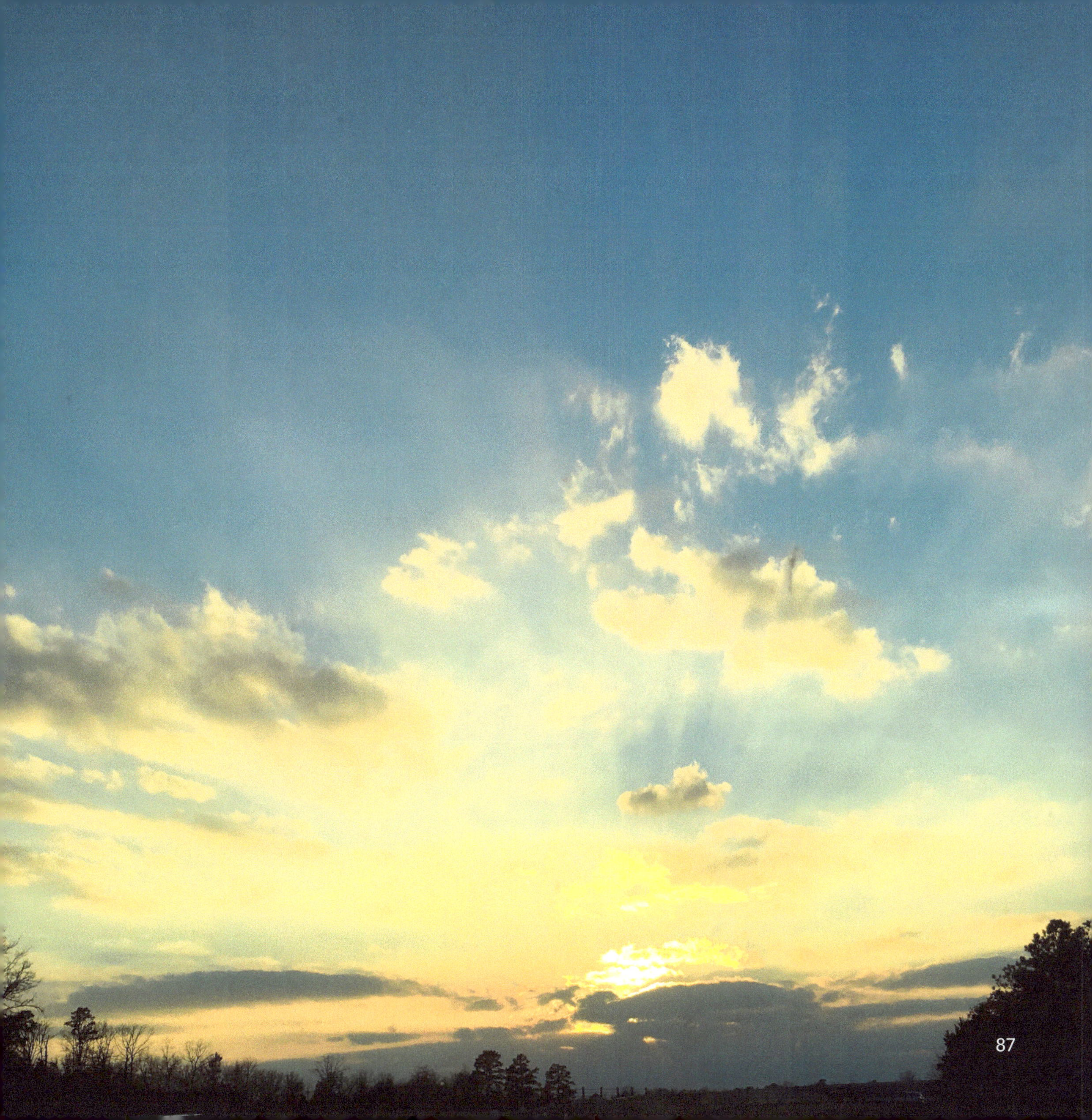

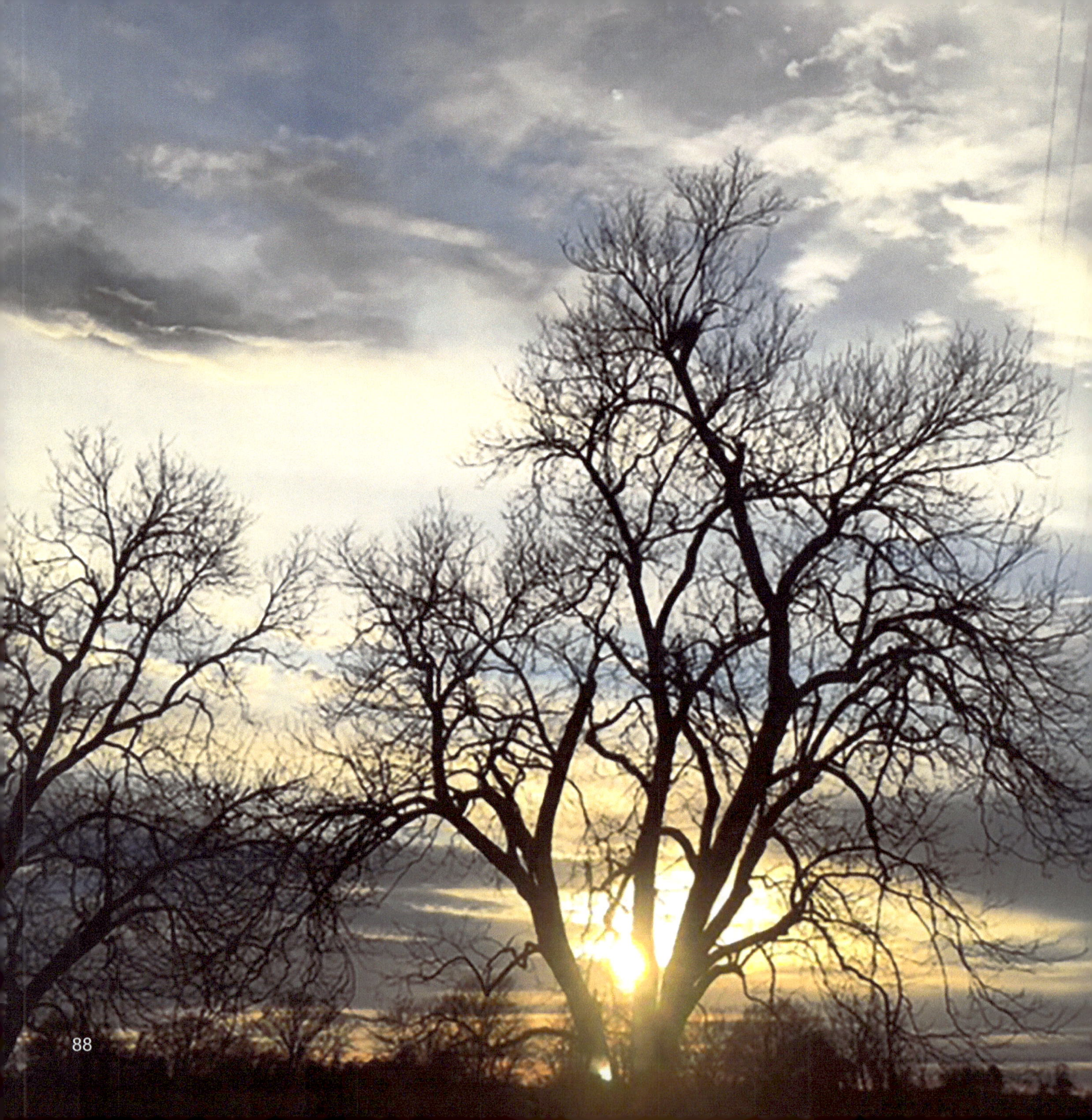

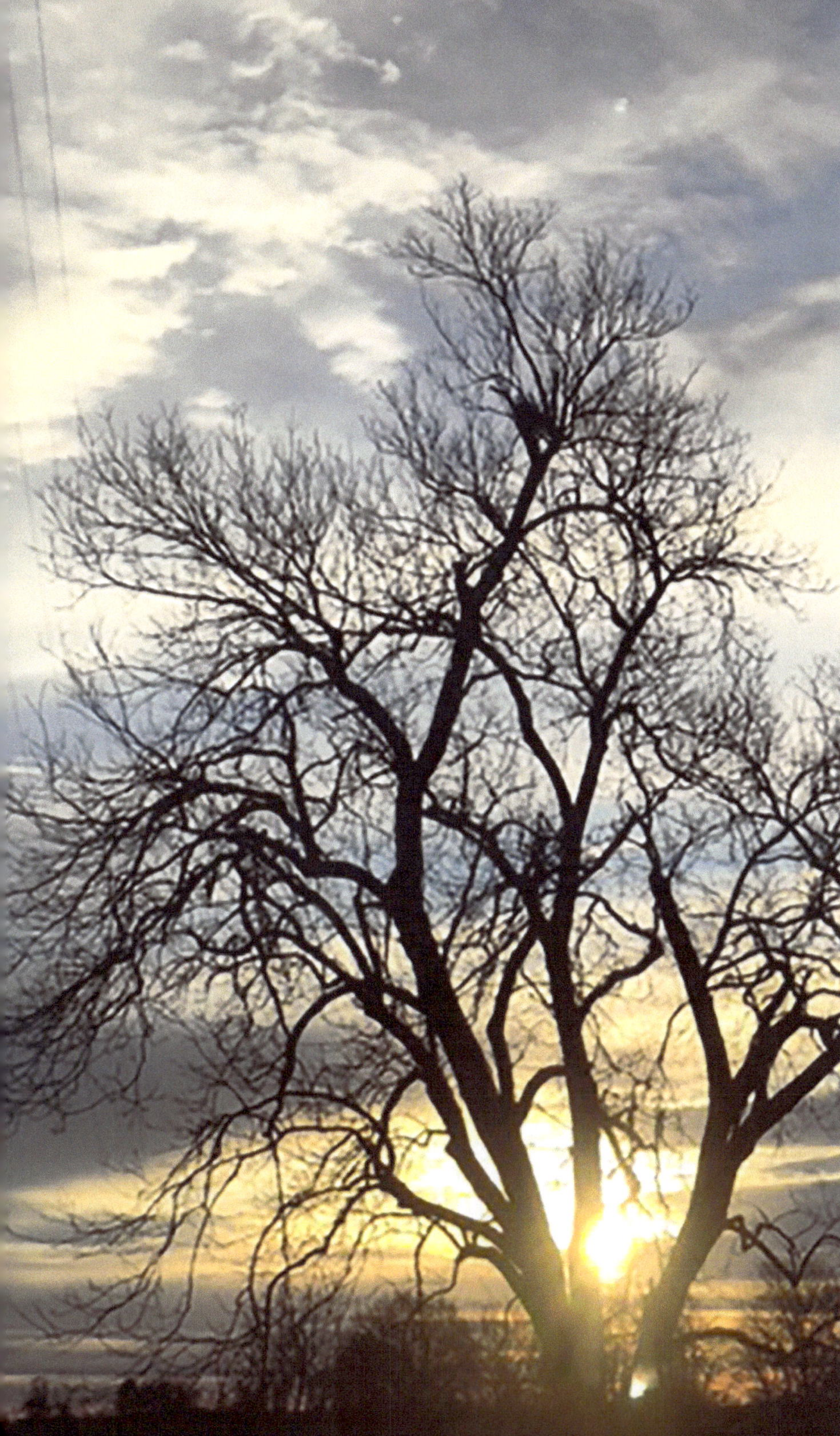

Find Peace

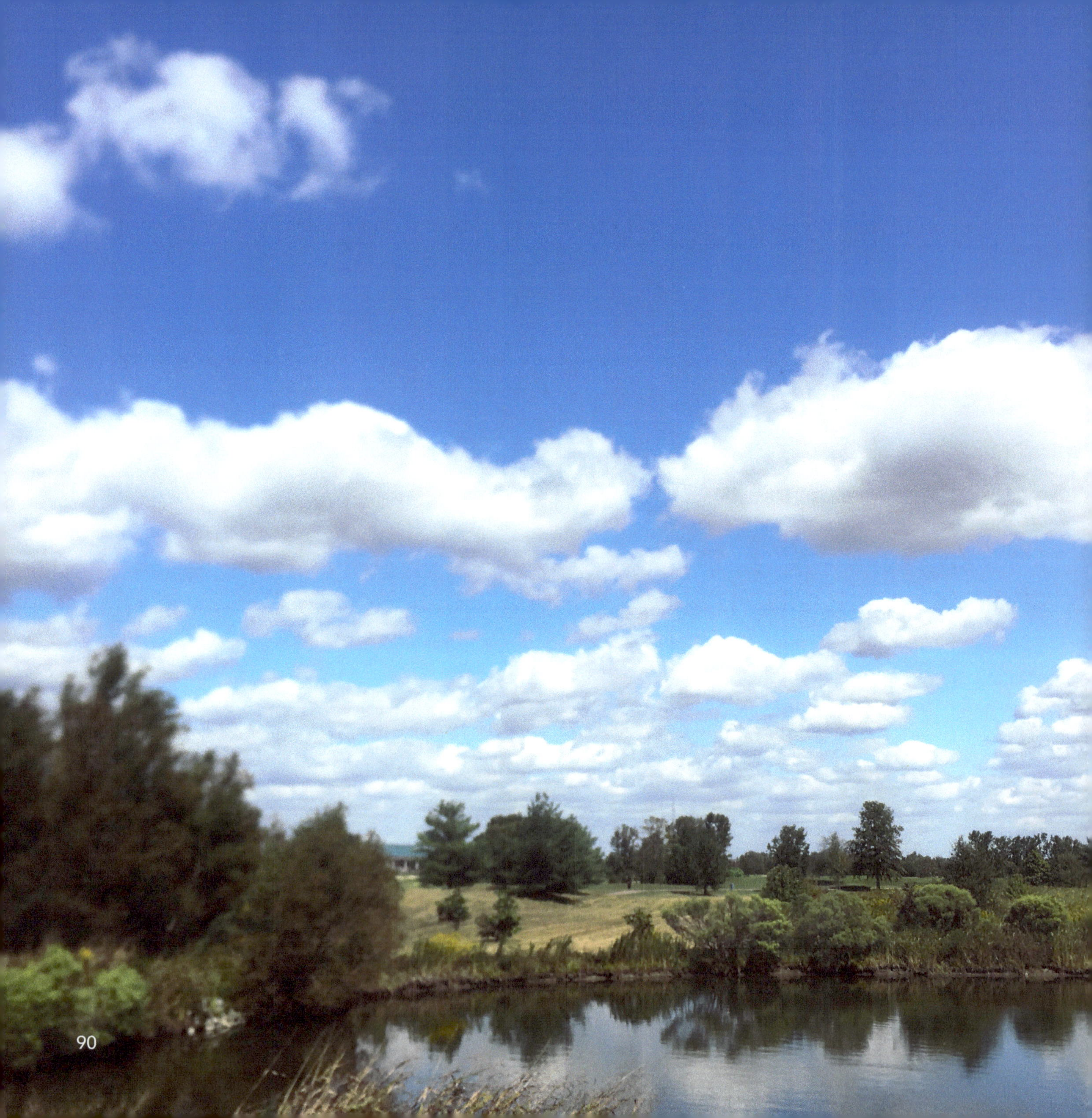

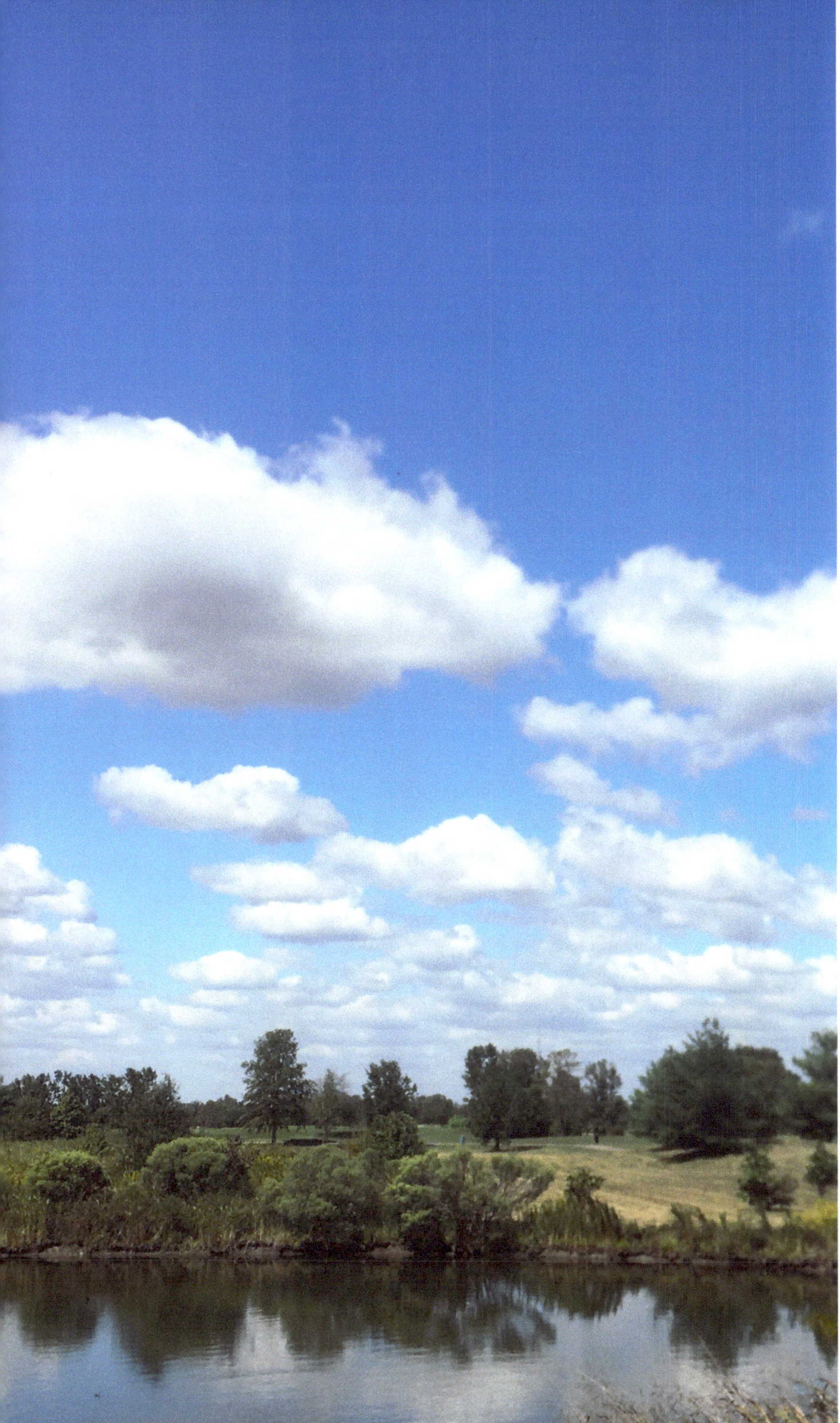

Golf Haven

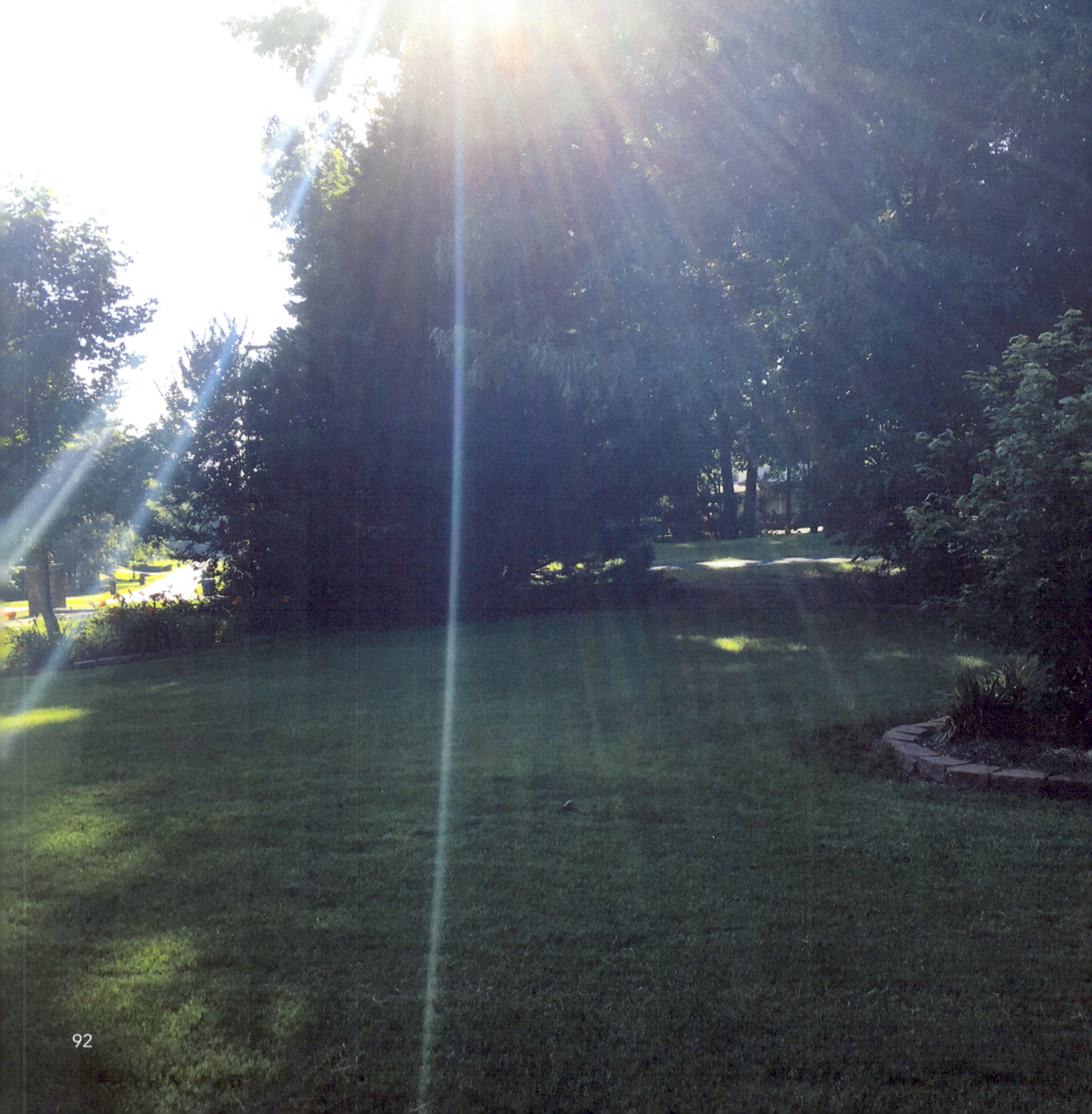

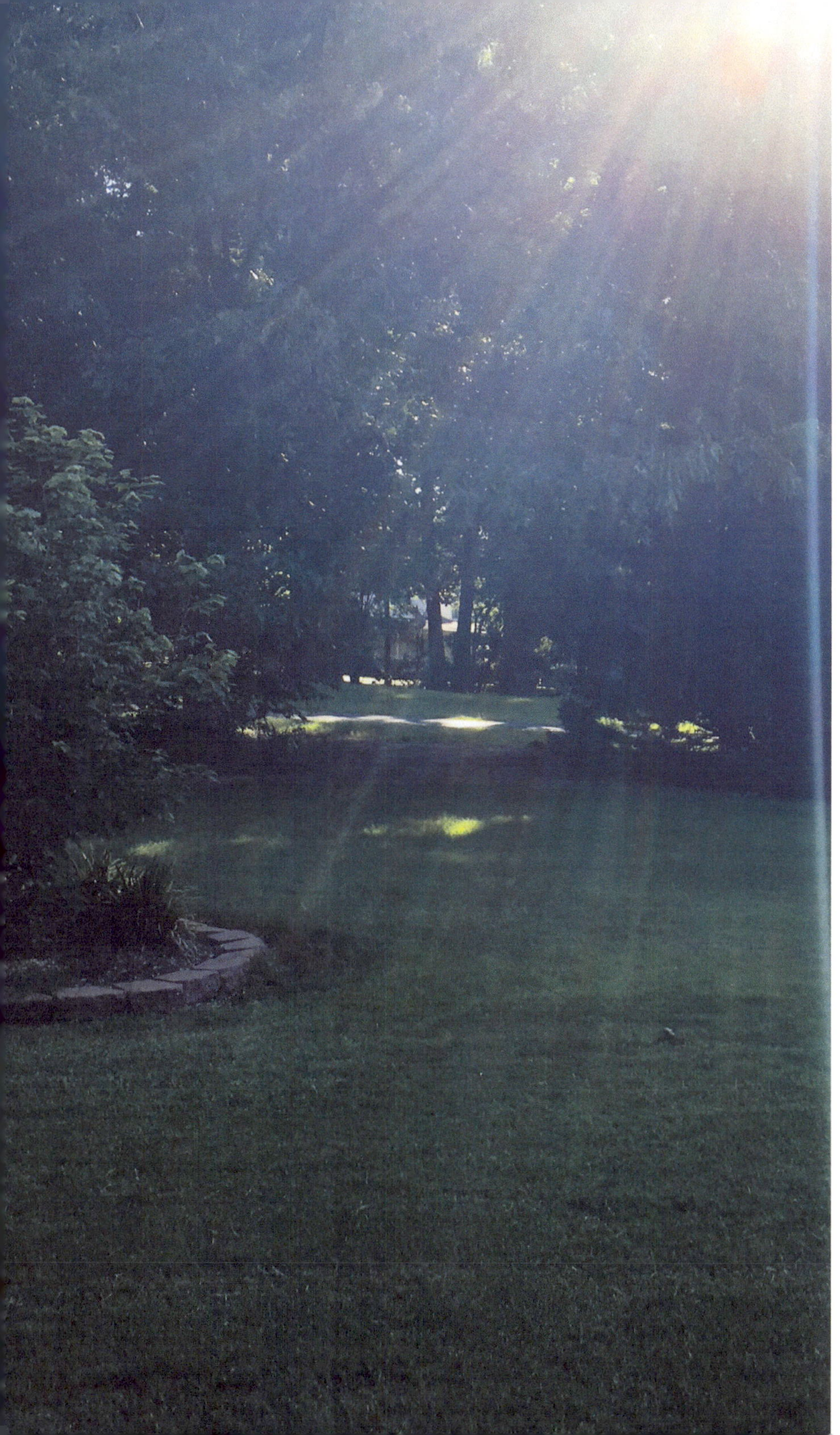

Backyard Blessing Beams

More About My Backyard Garden

***My** Backyard Garden, Look Up Mississippi* is an inspirational picture book. It is the second book published under the My Backyard Garden book series.

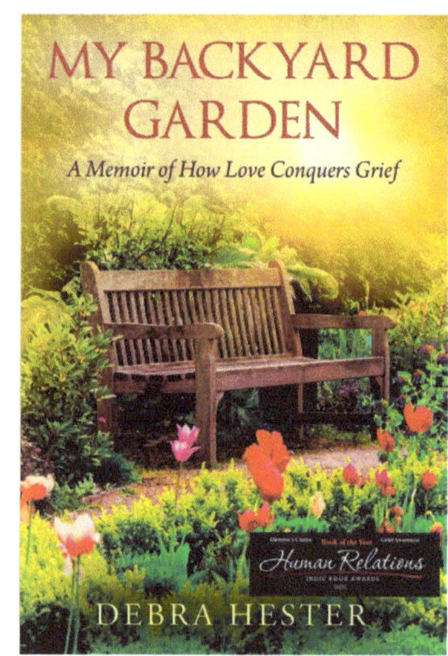

The first is ***My Backyard Garden, A Memoir of How Love Conquers Grief*** by Debra Hester. We look forward to sharing more inspiration and encouragement through My Backyard Garden books.

If you found peace and reflection in this book, we think you will enjoy the podcast that was inspired by the book: #empathyforgrief - Break the Silent Struggle With Grief Episode #19 - "Consolences In the Clouds."

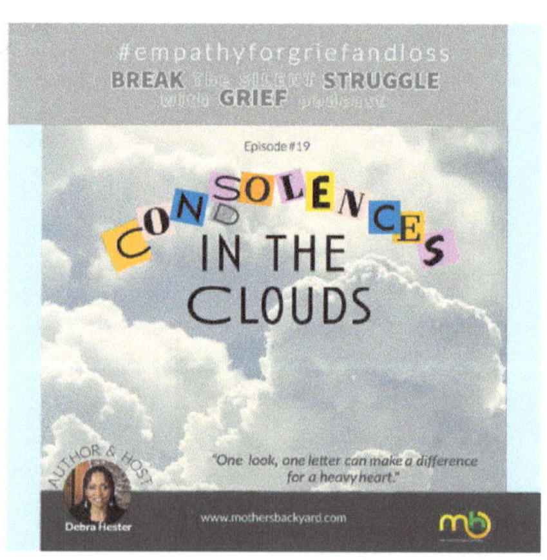

Available through most podcast providers and at:

www.mothersbackyard.org/backyard-buzz/

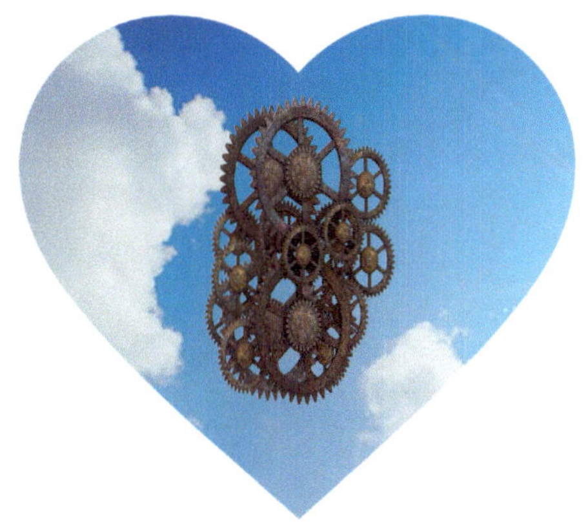

About the Author

Debra Hester is a creative, social entrepreneur and award-winning author. As the founder and CEO of MB Enterprises, her firm creates and provides educational and informational resources and experiences that inspire, inform, and transform. She has over 25 years' experience as a creative, innovative, HR, learning, and development global, senior-level leader. Debra loves to combine her journalism background to create engaging, visual, educational products and services.

A native of Arkansas, Debra grew up riding her bike in Catholic Hollow and along the Mississippi River levee in Helena, Arkansas. She also grew to realize the reputation of the land she loved as she worked and traveled globally. After 30 years away, Debra returned because she remembered the natural beauty of the Mississippi-Arkansas Delta. *Look Up Mississippi* is her way of documenting a positive response to this historic step forward. "*Look Up Mississippi* is a reminder to us all that this God-given beauty binds us together. And we must embrace this blessing and look for opportunities to experience peace and unity."

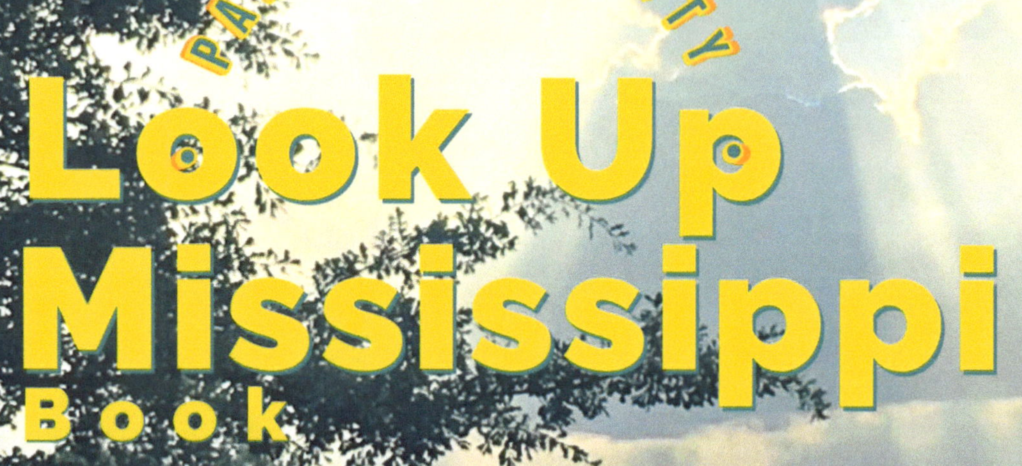

We offer a "special" paint and activity version of this book. Fun for all ages. Learn more at www.mbehrdevelopment.com

Look Up Mississippi

Paint & Trivia Book

We offer "special" paint versions of this book.
Fun for all ages. Learn more at
www.mbehrdevelopment.com